First Edition

W9-BIE-402

triumphlearning™
Common Core Coach
Mathematics 8

Dr. Jerry Kaplan
Senior Mathematics Consultant

Common Core Coach, Mathematics, First Edition, Grade 8 T119NA ISBN-13: 978-1-61997-441-8
Contributing Writers: Russell Kahn, Colleen O'Donnell Oppenzato **Cover Design:** Q2A/Bill Smith **Cover Illustration:** Carl Wiens

Triumph Learning® 136 Madison Avenue, 7th Floor, New York, NY 10016 © 2013 Triumph Learning, LLC. Buckle Down and Coach are imprints of Triumph Learning. All rights reserved. No part of this publication may be reproduced in whole or in part, stored in a retrieval system, or transmitted in any form or by any means, electronic, mechanical, photocopying, recording or otherwise, without written permission from the publisher.

Printed in the United States of America. 10 9 8 7 6 5 4 3 2 1

The National Governors Association Center for Best Practices and Council of Chief State School Officers are the sole owners and developers of the Common Core State Standards, © Copyright 2010. All rights reserved.

Contents

Problem
Solving

Performance
Task

Grade 7 NS

Apply and extend previous understandings of operations with fractions to add, subtract, multiply, and divide rational numbers.

Grade 8 NS

Know that there are numbers that are not rational, and approximate them by rational numbers.

Domain 1
The Number System

LESSON 1
Understanding Rational and Irrational Numbers

UNDERSTAND All numbers can be written with a decimal point. For example, you can rewrite −2 and 5 with decimal points without changing their values.

$-2 = -2.0$ or -2.00 or -2.000, and so on

$5 = 5.0$ or 5.00 or 5.000, and so on

You can expand the decimal places of a number that already has digits to the right of the decimal point.

$-2.2 = -2.20$ or -2.200, and so on

$5.\overline{1} = 5.1\overline{1}$ or $5.11\overline{1}$, and so on

Each of the numbers above has a decimal expansion that ends either in zeros or in a repeating digit. Any number with a decimal expansion that ends in 0s or in repeating decimal digits is a **rational number**.

UNDERSTAND Some numbers, like the ones below, do not end in 0s or in repeating decimal digits. The three dots, called an ellipsis, mean that digits continue, but not in a repeating pattern.

$\sqrt{2} = 1.41421...$ $\qquad$ $\sqrt{5} = 2.23606...$ $\qquad$ $-\sqrt{10} = -3.16227...$

Any number with a decimal expansion that does not end in 0s or in repeating decimal digits is an **irrational number**. You have previously worked with a very important number, pi, which is represented by the symbol π.

$\pi = 3.14159...$

The decimal expansion of π does not end in 0s or in repeating decimal digits. It is an irrational number.

Every **real number** belongs either to the set of rational numbers or to the set of irrational numbers.

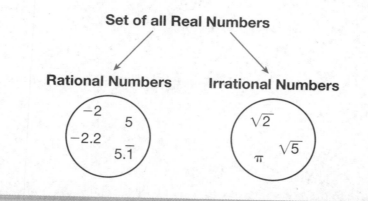

⊸ Connect

Is 0.07 rational or irrational?

> Examine the digits to the right of the decimal point.
>
> 0.07 = 0.070 or 0.0700, and so on
>
> 0.07 is rational because its decimal expansion ends in 0s.

Is $3.\overline{45}$ rational or irrational?

> Examine the digits to the right of the decimal point.
>
> $3.\overline{45}$ = $3.45\overline{45}$ or $3.4545\overline{45}$, and so on
>
> $3.\overline{45}$ is rational because its decimal expansion repeats.

Is 10.049846... rational or irrational?

> Examine the digits to the right of the decimal point.
>
> 10.049846...
>
> 10.049846... is irrational because its decimal expansion does not end in 0s or in repeating decimal digits.

Is $\sqrt{8}$ rational or irrational?

> Use a calculator to find the decimal form.
>
> $\sqrt{8}$ = 2.828427125...
>
> Examine the digits to the right of the decimal point.
>
> $\sqrt{8}$ is irrational because its decimal expansion does not end in 0s or in repeating decimal digits.

DISCUSS

How could you show that 4.95271 is a rational number using methods shown above?

EXAMPLE A Write each of the following rational numbers in fraction form.

3, −0.9, 3.03

1

Express each number as a fraction of the form $\frac{a}{b}$ where a and b are integers and $b \neq 0$.
Use the place value of the rightmost digit to determine the value of the denominator.

The rightmost digit in 3 is in the ones place, so $3 = \frac{3}{1}$.

The rightmost digit in −0.9 is in the tenths place, so $-0.9 = -\frac{9}{10}$.

The rightmost digit in 3.03 is in the hundredths place, so $3.03 = \frac{303}{100}$.

2

▶ $3 = \frac{3}{1}$ $-0.9 = -\frac{9}{10}$ $3.03 = \frac{303}{100}$

EXAMPLE B Convert the rational number $0.\overline{3}$ to a fraction.

1

Use algebra.
Set the number, $0.\overline{3}$, equal to n.

$n = 0.\overline{3}$

There is one repeating digit, so multiply n by the first power of 10, or 10.

$10n = 3.\overline{3}$

2

Subtract the number, n, from $10n$.

$$\begin{array}{r} 10n = 3.\overline{3} \\ -\quad n = 0.\overline{3} \\ \hline 9n = 3 \end{array}$$

3

Solve the equation and simplify the result.

$\frac{9n}{9} = \frac{3}{9}$

$n = \frac{3}{9}$

$ = \frac{1}{3}$

▶ $0.\overline{3} = \frac{1}{3}$

CHECK

How can you work backward from $\frac{1}{3}$ to check the answer?

EXAMPLE C Convert $0.\overline{45}$ to a fraction.

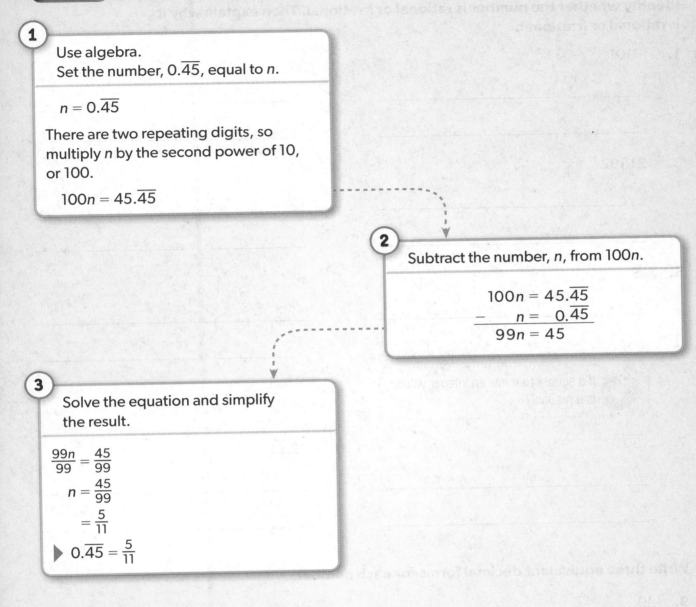

1

Use algebra.
Set the number, $0.\overline{45}$, equal to n.

$n = 0.\overline{45}$

There are two repeating digits, so multiply n by the second power of 10, or 100.

$100n = 45.\overline{45}$

2

Subtract the number, n, from $100n$.

$$100n = 45.\overline{45}$$
$$- \quad n = 0.\overline{45}$$
$$99n = 45$$

3

Solve the equation and simplify the result.

$$\frac{99n}{99} = \frac{45}{99}$$
$$n = \frac{45}{99}$$
$$= \frac{5}{11}$$

▶ $0.\overline{45} = \frac{5}{11}$

DISCUSS

What steps could you use to express the decimal $0.8\overline{3}$ as a fraction?

Practice

Identify whether the number is rational or irrational. Then explain why it is rational or irrational.

1. −101

    _____

    _____

2. $\frac{8}{17}$

    _____

    _____

3. 21.192

    _____

    _____

4. $\sqrt{7}$

    _____

    _____

5. $\sqrt{9}$

    _____

    _____

6. π

    _____

    _____

> HINT If a square root has an integer value, is it rational?

7. $\sqrt{50}$

    _____

    _____

8. $39.\overline{81}$

    _____

    _____

Write three equivalent decimal forms for each number.

9. 19 _____ _____ _____

10. 21.5 _____ _____ _____

11. −44.045 _____ _____ _____

> REMEMBER Adding zeros to the end of a decimal does not change its value.

12. $1.\overline{1}$ _____ _____ _____

Complete each sentence.

13. −11.3 is rational because _____.

14. $\sqrt{19}$ is irrational because _____.

15. $0.08\overline{3}$ is rational because _____.

16. 2.1371938... is irrational because _____.

Convert the repeating decimal to a fraction.

17. $0.\overline{6}$

18. $1.\overline{1}$

19. $4.\overline{4}$

_____   _____   _____

20. $9.\overline{09}$

21. $2.\overline{90}$

22. $4.\overline{54}$

_____   _____   _____

Choose the best answer.

23. Which is an irrational number?

    A. $-3.3\overline{4}$

    B. $\sqrt{1}$

    C. $\sqrt{20}$

    D. 11.2092

24. Which number is **not** equivalent to 13.02?

    A. 13.002

    B. 13.020

    C. 13.0200

    D. 13.020000

Solve.

25. **WRITE MATH** Convert $3.1\overline{6}$ to a fraction. Explain your strategy or show the steps you used to convert the number.

_____

_____

_____

26. **DESCRIBE** Describe two real-life applications of irrational numbers.

_____

_____

_____

Estimating the Value of Irrational Expressions

> **UNDERSTAND** All rational and irrational numbers can be represented by points on a number line. To find the location of an irrational number on a number line, you need to use a rational approximation.

Find the approximate location of $\sqrt{12}$ on a number line.

Identify the two closest integer values.

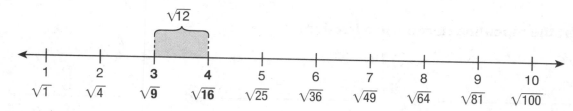

Identify the two closest decimal values to the tenths place. Because 12 is closer to 9 than to 16, $\sqrt{12}$ is closer to 3 than to 4. Compute the squares of 3.4 and 3.5 and compare the results to 12.

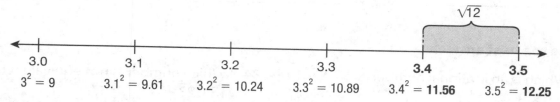

Identify the two closest decimal values to the hundredths place. Because 12 is closer to 12.25 than to 11.56, $\sqrt{12}$ is closer to 3.5 than to 3.4. Compute the squares of 3.46 and 3.47 and compare the results to 12.

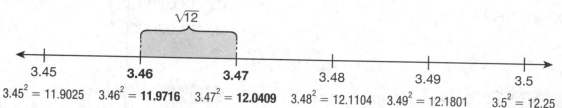

Because 12 is closer to 11.9716 than to 12.0409, $\sqrt{12}$ is closer to 3.46 than to 3.47.

You can approximate $\sqrt{12}$ on a number line as a point located between 3.46 and 3.47, closer to 3.46.

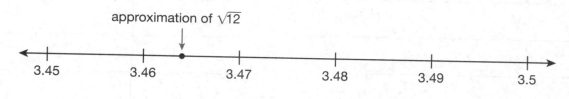

← Connect

Find a rational approximation of $\sqrt{8}$ to the nearest thousandth.

1 Identify the closest integers.

4 and 9 are perfect squares and
$4 < 8 < 9$.
$$\sqrt{4} = 2 \qquad \sqrt{9} = 3$$
$\sqrt{4} < \sqrt{8} < \sqrt{9}$, so $2 < \sqrt{8} < 3$.

2 Identify the closest tenths.

Because 8 is closer to 9 than to 4,
$\sqrt{8}$ is closer to 3 than to 2.

Investigate the squares of decimals that are closer to 3.
$$2.6^2 = 6.76 \qquad 2.7^2 = 7.29$$
$$2.8^2 = \textbf{7.84} \quad \leftarrow \quad \text{8 is greater than 7.84}$$
$$2.9^2 = \textbf{8.41} \quad \leftarrow \quad \text{8 is less than 8.41}$$
Therefore, $2.8 < \sqrt{8} < 2.9$.

3 Identify the closest hundredths.

Because 8 is closer to 7.84 than to 8.41,
$\sqrt{8}$ is closer to 2.8 than to 2.9.

Investigate the squares of decimals that are closer to 2.8.
$$2.80^2 = 7.84 \qquad 2.81^2 = 7.8961$$
$$2.82^2 = \textbf{7.9524} \quad \leftarrow \quad \text{8 is greater than 7.9524}$$
$$2.83^2 = \textbf{8.0089} \quad \leftarrow \quad \text{8 is less than 8.0089}$$
Therefore, $2.82 < \sqrt{8} < 2.83$.

4 Identify the closest thousandths.

Because 8 is closer to 8.0089 than to 7.9524, $\sqrt{8}$ is closer to 2.83 than to 2.82.

Investigate the squares of decimals that are closer to 2.83.
$$2.827^2 = 7.991929$$
$$2.828^2 = \textbf{7.997584} \quad \leftarrow \quad \text{8 is greater than 7.997584}$$
$$2.829^2 = \textbf{8.003241} \quad \leftarrow \quad \text{8 is less than 8.003241}$$
Therefore, $2.828 < \sqrt{8} < 2.829$.

5 Because 8 is closer to 7.997584 than to 8.003241, $\sqrt{8}$ is closer to 2.828 than to 2.829.

▶ A rational approximation of $\sqrt{8}$ to the nearest thousandth is 2.828.

TRY

Find the rational approximation of $\sqrt{7}$ to the nearest tenth.

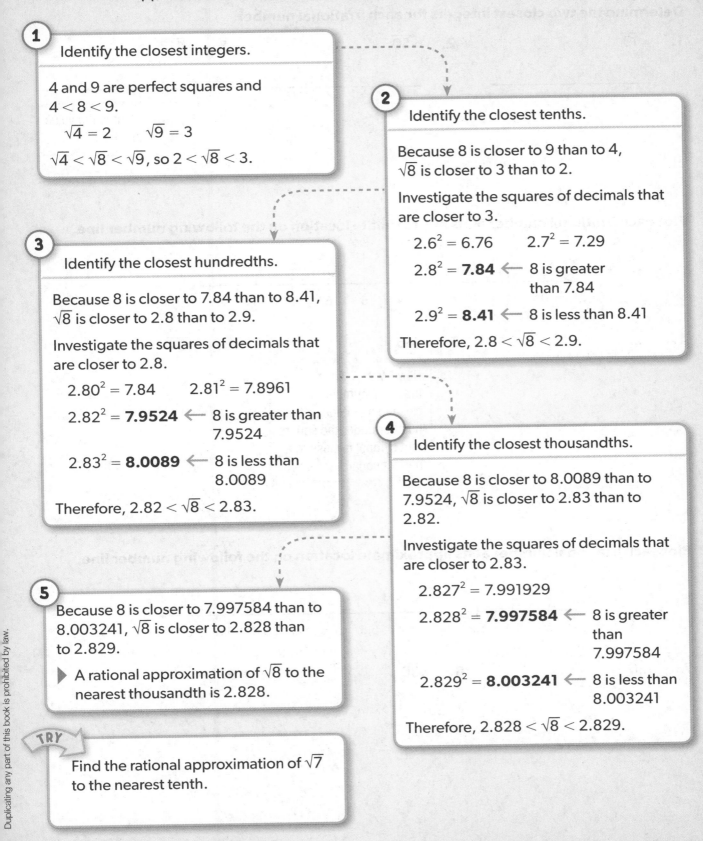

Practice

Determine the two closest integers for each irrational number.

1. $\sqrt{19}$

2. $\sqrt{50}$

3. $\sqrt{117}$

_____

_____

_____

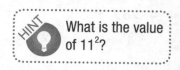
HINT What is the value of 11^2?

Plot each irrational number at its approximate location on the following number line.

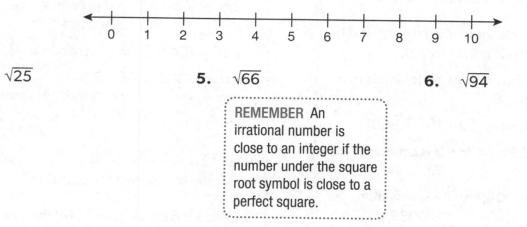

4. $\sqrt{25}$

5. $\sqrt{66}$

6. $\sqrt{94}$

REMEMBER An irrational number is close to an integer if the number under the square root symbol is close to a perfect square.

Plot each irrational number at its approximate location on the following number line.

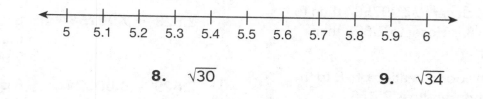

7. $\sqrt{26}$

8. $\sqrt{30}$

9. $\sqrt{34}$

Approximate the value of each irrational expression. Use $\frac{22}{7}$ as a rational approximation for π.

10. 2π

11. $5\pi + 1$

12. π^2

_____   _____   _____

Complete each sentence. Write decimals to the hundredths place.

13. $\sqrt{66}$ is between 8.12 and _____, and it is closer to _____.

14. $\sqrt{85}$ is between _____ and _____, and it is closer to _____.

15. $\sqrt{97}$ is between _____ and _____, and it is closer to _____.

Choose the best answer.

16. Which is the best approximation for $\sqrt{3}$?

    A. 1.7

    B. 1.73

    C. 1.74

    D. 1.8

17. Which is the best approximation for $\sqrt{102}$?

    A. 10

    B. 10.09

    C. 10.099

    D. 10.1

Solve.

18. WRITE MATH An architect needs two support beams for a building. One beam has a length of $2\sqrt{3}$ meters. Another has a length of $3\sqrt{2}$ meters. Explain how you can find which beam is longer.

_____

_____

_____

19. COMPARE Approximate $\sqrt{31}$ with a decimal to the nearest hundredth. How does the square of that approximation compare to 31?

_____

_____

_____

Choose the best answer.

1. Which number is irrational?

    A. $-\dfrac{213}{2}$

    B. $3.1\overline{2}$

    C. $\sqrt{64}$

    D. $9.31307\ldots$

2. Which is the best approximation for $\sqrt{55}$?

    A. 7

    B. 7.41

    C. 7.42

    D. 8

3. Plot $\sqrt{51}$ on the following number line.

Complete each sentence.

4. $\sqrt{144}$ is rational because _____.

5. 10π is irrational because _____.

Approximate each number to the nearest tenth.

6. $\sqrt{90}$ **7.** $\sqrt{71}$ **8.** $\sqrt{72}$

_____   _____   _____

Write each decimal as a fraction.

9. $0.\overline{8}$ **10.** $0.\overline{89}$ **11.** $0.8\overline{6}$

_____   _____   _____

Choose the best answer.

12. Which number is rational?

    A. $-\sqrt{9}$

    B. 0.010010001…

    C. $\sqrt{65}$

    D. $\sqrt{-100}$

13. Which is the best approximation for $\sqrt{44}$?

    A. 6.6

    B. 6.63

    C. 6.64

    D. 7

14. Plot $\sqrt{6}$ on the following number line.

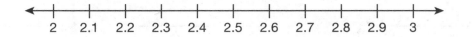

15. Plot $\sqrt{47}$ on the following number line.

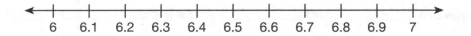

16. Plot $-\sqrt{77}$ on the following number line.

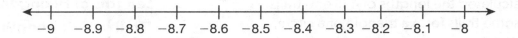

Write three equivalent decimals for each number.

17. −132   _____   _____   _____

18. 93.3   _____   _____   _____

19. 0.09   _____   _____   _____

20. −4.2323   _____   _____   _____

Write each decimal as a fraction.

21. $0.\overline{3}$

_____

22. $2.\overline{2}$

_____

23. $0.\overline{18}$

_____

24. $3.6\overline{3}$

_____

25. $2.\overline{90}$

_____

26. $9.\overline{7}$

_____

Determine the two closest integers for each irrational number.

27. $\sqrt{88}$

_____

28. $\sqrt{5}$

_____

29. $\sqrt{27}$

_____

Complete each sentence. Write decimals to the hundredths place.

30. $\sqrt{33}$ is between 5.74 and _____, and it is closer to _____.

31. $\sqrt{11}$ is between _____ and _____, and it is closer to _____.

32. $\sqrt{105}$ is between _____ and _____, and it is closer to _____.

Use the situation and table to answer questions 33 and 34.

Carissa calculated the lengths of 4 hiking trails. Because some trails form a triangle or a circle, some lengths have square roots or the π symbol.

Lengths of Hiking Trails

Trail	Length (in km)
Valley View	$2.5\sqrt{4}$
Butterfly Gulch	2π
Waterfall Perch	4.275
Forest Walk	$2\sqrt{5}$

33. **IDENTIFY** Identify the trails that have irrational lengths. Explain your reasoning.

_____

_____

_____

34. **LIST** List the lengths from shortest to longest. Explain your work.

_____

_____

_____

Approximating Circumference

For this activity, you will need a ruler, string, and a variety of circular flat objects, such as coins, CDs, plastic lids, etc.

Use a ruler to measure the diameter of each of your circular objects. Fill in the following table to show the diameters and estimate the circumference of each object.

Object	Diameter	Actual Circumference (including π)	Approximate Circumference

Is the actual circumference of each object rational or irrational? Explain.

_____

_____

Is the approximate circumference of each object rational or irrational? Explain.

_____

_____

Cut a piece of string based on the approximate circumference for each object. Wrap the corresponding string around each object to determine whether it accurately measures the distance around it.

Explain whether the lengths of your string match the circumference of the circular object. Did the approximations help you find accurate lengths for the strings?

_____

_____

_____

Grade 7

Grade 8

Grade 7 RP

Analyze proportional relationships and use them to solve real-world and mathematical problems.

Grade 7 NS

Apply and extend previous understandings of operations with fractions to add, subtract, multiply, and divide rational numbers.

Grade 7 EE

Use properties of operations to generate equivalent expressions.

Solve real-life and mathematical problems using numerical and algebraic expressions and equations.

Grade 8 EE

Work with radicals and integer exponents.

Understand the connections between proportional relationships, lines, and linear equations.

Analyze and solve linear equations and pairs of simultaneous linear equations.

Domain 2
Expressions and Equations

Applying Properties of Exponents

UNDERSTAND In an exponential expression such as 4^7, the number 4 is called the **base**. The number 7 is called the **exponent**. It tells how many times the base is used as a factor. So, $4^7 = 4 \times 4 \times 4 \times 4 \times 4 \times 4 \times 4$. If the exponent is negative, put the exponential expression in the denominator of a fraction with a numerator of 1. So, $4^{-7} = \frac{1}{4^7}$.

$$5^3 = 5 \times 5 \times 5 = 125$$

base   exponent

$$5^{-3} = \frac{1}{5^3} = \frac{1}{5 \times 5 \times 5} = \frac{1}{125}$$

To multiply exponential expressions with the same bases, add the exponents.

$$5^3 \times 5^2 = 5^{3+2} = 5^5$$

Why this works:

$$5^3 \times 5^2 = (5 \times 5 \times 5) \times (5 \times 5)$$
$$= (5 \times 5 \times 5 \times 5 \times 5) = 5^5$$

To divide exponential expressions with the same bases, subtract the exponents.

$$\frac{4^5}{4^3} = 4^{5-3} = 4^2$$

Why this works:

$$\frac{4^5}{4^3} = \frac{4 \times 4 \times \cancel{4} \times \cancel{4} \times \cancel{4}}{\cancel{4} \times \cancel{4} \times \cancel{4}}$$
$$= \frac{4 \times 4}{1} = 4^2$$

To find the value of an exponential expression with an exponent, multiply the exponents.

$$(3^2)^3 = 3^{2 \times 3} = 3^6$$

Why this works:

$$(3^2)^3 = 3^2 \times 3^2 \times 3^2$$
$$= (3 \times 3) \times (3 \times 3) \times (3 \times 3)$$
$$= (3 \times 3 \times 3 \times 3 \times 3 \times 3) = 3^6$$

When a product has an exponent, the exponent applies to each factor.

$$(9x)^3 = (9^3)(x^3) = 729x^3$$

Why this works:

$$(9x)^3 = 9x \cdot 9x \cdot 9x$$
$$= (9 \cdot 9 \cdot 9)(x \cdot x \cdot x)$$
$$= 9^3 \cdot x^3 = 729x^3$$

When a quotient has an exponent, the exponent applies to each term.

$$\left(\frac{3}{4}\right)^3 = \frac{3^3}{4^3} = \frac{27}{64}$$

Why this works:

$$\left(\frac{3}{4}\right)^3 = \frac{3}{4} \cdot \frac{3}{4} \cdot \frac{3}{4} = \frac{3^3}{4^3} = \frac{3 \times 3 \times 3}{4 \times 4 \times 4} = \frac{27}{64}$$

⚡ Connect

Multiply: $7^6 \times 7^{-4}$

> The expressions have the same base, 7, so add the exponents and simplify.
>
> $7^6 \times 7^{-4} = 7^{6+(-4)}$
>
> $\qquad\qquad = 7^2$
>
> $\qquad\qquad = 7 \times 7$
>
> $\qquad\qquad = 49$
>
> ▶ $7^6 \times 7^{-4} = 49$

Divide: $\dfrac{3^{-2}}{3^3}$

> The expressions have the same base, 3, so subtract the exponents and simplify.
>
> $\dfrac{3^{-2}}{3^3} = 3^{-2-3}$
>
> $\qquad = 3^{-5}$
>
> $\qquad = \dfrac{1}{3^5}$
>
> $\qquad = \dfrac{1}{3 \times 3 \times 3 \times 3 \times 3}$
>
> $\qquad = \dfrac{1}{243}$
>
> ▶ $\dfrac{3^{-2}}{3^3} = \dfrac{1}{243}$

Evaluate: $(2^{-3})^2$

> The exponential expression has an exponent, so multiply the exponents. Then simplify.
>
> $(2^{-3})^2 = 2^{-3 \times 2}$
>
> $\qquad\quad = 2^{-6}$
>
> $\qquad\quad = \dfrac{1}{2^6}$
>
> $\qquad\quad = \dfrac{1}{2 \times 2 \times 2 \times 2 \times 2 \times 2}$
>
> $\qquad\quad = \dfrac{1}{64}$
>
> ▶ $(2^{-3})^2 = \dfrac{1}{64}$

Evaluate: $\left(\dfrac{2}{5}\right)^{-3}$

> Find the negative power of a quotient.
>
> $\left(\dfrac{2}{5}\right)^{-3} = \dfrac{2^{-3}}{5^{-3}}$
>
> $\qquad\quad = \dfrac{1}{2^3} \div \dfrac{1}{5^3}$
>
> $\qquad\quad = \dfrac{1}{2^3} \times \dfrac{5^3}{1}$
>
> $\qquad\quad = \dfrac{5^3}{2^3}$
>
> $\qquad\quad = \dfrac{5 \times 5 \times 5}{2 \times 2 \times 2}$
>
> $\qquad\quad = \dfrac{125}{8}$
>
> ▶ $\left(\dfrac{2}{5}\right)^{-3} = \dfrac{125}{8} = 15\dfrac{5}{8}$

DISCUSS

How can you write $\dfrac{2^{-5}}{7^{-2}}$ as an exponential expression with positive exponents?

Practice

Evaluate each expression. Leave your answer in exponential form.

1. $3^4 \times 3^2$

   _____

2. $9^7 \times 9^3$

   _____

3. $6^3 \times 6^3$

   _____

> **REMEMBER** You can multiply exponential expressions with like bases by adding the exponents.

4. $5^5 \times 5^4$

   _____

5. $1^{11} \times 1^{-9}$

   _____

6. $x^3 \times x^{-6}$

   _____

7. $\dfrac{4^9}{4^7}$

   _____

8. $\dfrac{2^{-10}}{2^4}$

   _____

9. $\dfrac{z^{20}}{z^{10}}$

   _____

Complete each sentence.

10. To evaluate $(4^3)^4$, I need to _____ the exponents.

11. To evaluate $\dfrac{10^6}{10^4}$, I need to _____ the exponents.

12. To evaluate $p^{-2} \times p^9$, I need to _____ the exponents.

Evaluate each expression. Write your answer in standard form.

13. $2^2 \times 2^3$

    _____

14. $3^3 \times 3^2$

    _____

15. $\dfrac{6^7}{6^5}$

    _____

16. $\dfrac{9^9}{9^8}$

    _____

17. $\left(\dfrac{1}{4}\right)^3$

    _____

18. $\left(\dfrac{4}{9}\right)^2$

    _____

Evaluate each expression. Write your answer in standard form. Justify each answer.

19. $5^{10} \times 5^{-7}$

_____

_____

20. $7^{-4} \times 7^{6}$

_____

_____

21. $\dfrac{2^{-5}}{2^{-8}}$

_____

_____

22. $\dfrac{10^{-11}}{10^{-10}}$

_____

_____

23. $1^{17} \times 1^{-8}$

_____

_____

24. $\left(\dfrac{2}{3}\right)^{-3}$

_____

_____

Choose the best answer.

25. Which expression is equal to $\dfrac{13^{-11}}{13^{-12}}$?

   A. 13^{-23}

   B. 13^{-1}

   C. 13

   D. 13^{132}

26. Which expression is equal to $(5^4)^{-3}$?

   A. 5^{-12}

   B. 5^{-7}

   C. 5

   D. 5^{12}

Solve.

27. **CHOOSE** Choose a rational approximation for π. Then evaluate $\dfrac{\pi^7}{\pi^5}$.

_____

_____

_____

28. **RESTATE** In your own words, explain how you know that $(d^6)^2$ is equal to d^{12}.

_____

_____

_____

LESSON 4

Understanding Square and Cube Roots

UNDERSTAND x is the **square root** of a nonnegative number n if $x^2 = n$. For example, 7 is the square root of 49 because $7^2 = 49$. It is also true that -7 is the square root of 49 because $-7^2 = 49$. However, we define the **principal square root**, represented by the $\sqrt{}$ symbol, as the positive number. So, while 7 and -7 are both square roots of 49, the principal square root of 49, or $\sqrt{49}$, is 7.

How do you solve an equation with a variable squared such as $x^2 = 100$?
You can solve this equation by finding what number multiplied by itself equals 100.

$x^2 = 100$ ← 100 is a perfect square, so $10 \times 10 = 100$ and $-10 \times -10 = 100$

$x = \pm\sqrt{100}$

$x = \pm 10$

Notice that $x^2 = 100$ has two solutions, -10 and 10, while $\sqrt{100} = 10$ because the principal square root is only the positive number.

If x^2 is not equal to a perfect square, then the solutions will be irrational numbers.

$x^2 = 5$ ← 5 is not a perfect square.

$x = \pm\sqrt{5}$

$x = \pm 2.23606\ldots$ (not a repeating decimal)

UNDERSTAND x is the **cube root** of a number n if $x^3 = n$. The symbol for cube root is $\sqrt[3]{}$.

$4 \times 4 \times 4 = 64$ so $\sqrt[3]{64} = 4$

The cube root can be a negative number.

$-5 \times -5 \times -5 = -125$ so $\sqrt[3]{-125} = -5$

You can solve an equation in which the variable is cubed by finding what number when used as a factor 3 times equals the given cube.

$x^3 = 343$

$x = \sqrt[3]{343}$ ← $7 \times 7 \times 7 = 343$

$x = 7$

⊷ Connect

Solve for x.

$x^2 = 169$

1

Find what number multiplied by itself equals 169.

$x^2 = 169$ Think: $13 \times 13 = 169$
and $-13 \times -13 = 169$

2

Solve the equation for x.

$x^2 = 169$ ← $13 \times 13 = 169$
and $-13 \times -13 = 169$

$x = \pm\sqrt{169}$

▶ $x = \pm 13$

Solve for x.

$x^3 = 216$

1

Find the product of three repeated factors equal to 216.

$x^3 = 216$ Think: $x \times x \times x = 216$

2

Solve for x.

$x^3 = 216$ ← $6 \times 6 \times 6 = 216$

$x = \sqrt[3]{216}$

▶ $x = 6$

TRY

Solve for x: $x^2 = \frac{16}{81}$. Justify your answer.

Practice

Find the principal square root.

1. $\sqrt{1}$

_____

2. $\sqrt{64}$

_____

3. $\sqrt{144}$

_____

4. $\sqrt{121}$

_____

5. $\sqrt{289}$

_____

6. $\sqrt{225}$

_____

Find the cube root.

7. $\sqrt[3]{1}$

_____

8. $\sqrt[3]{512}$

_____

9. $\sqrt[3]{-8}$

_____

10. $\sqrt[3]{125}$

_____

11. $\sqrt[3]{-729}$

_____

12. $\sqrt[3]{-1,000}$

_____

Solve the equation for x.

13. $x^2 = 1$

_____

_____

14. $x^2 = 256$

_____

_____

15. $x^3 = 0$

_____

_____

16. $x^2 = 225$

_____

_____

17. $x^2 = 0$

_____

_____

18. $x^3 = 27$

_____

_____

19. $x^2 = \dfrac{4}{36}$

_____

_____

20. $x^2 = \dfrac{16}{49}$

_____

_____

21. $x^3 = \dfrac{8}{27}$

_____

_____

22. $x^2 = 2.25$

_____

_____

23. $x^2 = 0.49$

_____

_____

24. $x^3 = 0.027$

_____

_____

Find each missing number.

25. $\sqrt{\square} = 5$

_____

26. $\sqrt[3]{\square} = 5$

_____

27. $\sqrt[3]{\square} = 10$

_____

Choose the best answer.

28. Which set shows all the solutions for $\sqrt[3]{64}$?

   A. 4 only

   B. −4 and 4

   C. 8 only

   D. −8 and 8

29. Which is the solution for $x^3 = -343$?

   A. $\sqrt[3]{7}$

   B. −7

   C. 7

   D. ±7

Solve.

30. **EXPLAIN** What is the principal square root of 36? Explain.

_____

_____

_____

31. **COMPARE** Compare the values of $\sqrt{1}$ and $\sqrt[3]{1}$. Explain how the values are similar or different.

_____

_____

_____

Scientific Notation

LESSON **5**

UNDERSTAND **Scientific notation** is a way to express very large and very small numbers. A number in scientific notation is the product of two factors: the first factor, called the **coefficient**, is a number less than 10 and greater than or equal to 1; the second factor is a power of 10.

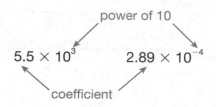

To convert a number in standard form to scientific notation, first move the decimal point to form the coefficient. Then multiply it by 10 with an exponent. The exponent will be the number of places the decimal point moves to make the coefficient. Numbers greater than or equal to 10 have positive exponents; numbers less than 1 have negative exponents.

What is 6,000,000,000 in scientific notation?

Locate the decimal and move it to the left. Stop before the first digit.

$$6.\underbrace{000000000.}_{+9}$$

Rewrite 6,000,000,000 as the product of a coefficient and a power of 10.

The decimal point moved 9 places.
6,000,000,000 is greater than 10, so the exponent is positive 9.

$6,000,000,000 = 6 \times 10^9$

What is 0.000015 in scientific notation?

Locate the decimal point and move it to the right. Stop after the first nonzero digit.

$$0.\underbrace{00001}_{-5}.5$$

Rewrite 0.000015 as the product of a coefficient and a power of 10.

0.000015 is rewritten as 1.5.
The decimal point moved 5 places.
0.000015 is less than 1, so the exponent is -5.

$0.000015 = 1.5 \times 10^{-5}$

⊸ Connect

The distance from Annabelle's house to her best friend's house is 2×10^2 km. The distance from Annabelle's house to her pen pal's house is 8×10^3 km. How many times the distance to her best friend's house is the distance to her pen pal's house?

1 Divide the distance to Annabelle's pen pal's house by the distance to her best friend's house.

$$\frac{8 \times 10^3}{2 \times 10^2}$$

2 Divide the coefficients.

$$8 \div 2 = 4$$

Divide the powers of 10.

$$10^3 \div 10^2 = 10^{3-2} = 10^1 = 10$$

3 Multiply the quotient of the coefficients by the quotient of the powers of 10.

$$4 \times 10 = 40$$

▶ The distance to the pen pal's house is 40 times the distance to the best friend's house.

The population of City A is 8×10^3. The population of City B is 4×10^6. How many times the population of City A is the population of City B?

1 To solve the problem, divide the population of City B by the population of City A.

$$\frac{4 \times 10^6}{8 \times 10^3}$$

Divide the coefficients.

$$4 \div 8 = 0.5$$

Divide the powers of 10.

$$10^6 \div 10^3 = 10^{6-3} = 10^3 = 1,000$$

2 Multiply the quotient of the coefficients and the quotient of the powers of 10.

$$0.5 \times 1,000 = 500$$

▶ The population of City B is 500 times the population of City A.

DISCUSS

2.7×10^4 is how many times as great as 2.7×10^{-4}? Explain how you can find the answer without computing.

Practice

Express each number in scientific notation.

1. 3,000

_____

2. 500,000

_____

3. 325,000

_____

HINT

If the decimal point moves left until just after the first digit, what coefficient will be formed?

4. 0.09

_____

5. 0.00004

_____

6. 0.00558

_____

Express each number in standard form.

7. 4×10^3

_____

8. 7.7×10^5

_____

9. 6.004×10^7

_____

10. 3×10^{-1}

_____

11. 2.19×10^{-2}

_____

12. 4.0805×10^{-3}

_____

Complete each sentence. Show your work.

13. 4.5×10^9 is _____ times as great as 4.5×10^5.

14. 9×10^5 is _____ times as great as 3×10^4.

15. 2×10^4 is _____ times as great as 5×10^3.

Complete each sentence. Show your work.

16. 7×10^{-2} is _____ times as great as 7×10^{-5}.

17. 5×10^{-1} is _____ times as great as 4×10^{-7}.

18. 2.5×10^{-3} is _____ times as great as 7.5×10^{-8}.

Choose the best answer.

19. The speed of light is about 300,000,000 meters per second. Which expression shows this speed in scientific notation?

   A. 300×10^3 m/s

   B. 30×10^6 m/s

   C. 3×10^8 m/s

   D. 3×10^9 m/s

20. The thickness of a human hair can be about 6×10^{-3} centimeters. Which shows this thickness in standard form?

   A. 0.06 cm

   B. 0.060 cm

   C. 0.006 cm

   D. 0.0006 cm

Solve.

21. A pronghorn antelope can travel at a speed of 6×10^1 miles per hour. A snail can travel at a speed of 3×10^{-2} miles per hour. How many times the speed of a snail is the speed of a pronghorn antelope?

_____

22. The mass of Mercury is about 3.3×10^{23} kg. The mass of Jupiter is about 1.9×10^{27} kg. About how many times the mass of Mercury is the mass of Jupiter?

_____

23. COMPUTE The weight of a gallon of water is about 8.345 pounds. Express the number in scientific notation, explaining how the exponent works in the expression.

_____

_____

_____

24. COMPARE Without converting the numbers to standard form, explain how you know which is greater: 5×10^{-5} or 6×10^{-6}?

_____

_____

_____

Duplicating any part of this book is prohibited by law.

Lesson 5: Scientific Notation **33**

LESSON 6 · Using Scientific Notation

EXAMPLE A Multiply: $(3.5 \times 10^3)(2 \times 10^5)$. Express the answer in scientific notation.

1

Multiplication is commutative and associative.
Rearrange the factors and group the coefficients and powers of 10.

$(3.5 \times 10^3)(2 \times 10^5) = (3.5 \times 2.0)(10^3 \times 10^5)$

2

Multiply the coefficients. Then multiply the powers of 10.

$(3.5 \times 2.0) = 7$

$(10^3 \times 10^5) = 10^{3+5} = 10^8$

3

Write the product in scientific notation.

7×10^8

▶ $(3.5 \times 10^3)(2 \times 10^5) = 7 \times 10^8$

EXAMPLE B Divide: $\dfrac{8 \times 10^6}{2.5 \times 10^3}$. Express the answer in standard form.

1

Divide the coefficients. Then divide the powers of 10.

$8 \div 2.5 = 3.2$

$10^6 \div 10^3 = 10^{6-3} = 10^3$

2

Express the answer in standard form.

$3.2 \times 10^3 = 3,200$

▶ $\dfrac{8 \times 10^6}{2.5 \times 10^3} = 3,200$

TRY

Express the quotient $\dfrac{9 \times 10^2}{3 \times 10^4}$ in standard form.

EXAMPLE C Use a calculator to multiply: $(2.3 \times 10^5)(6.4 \times 10^7)$

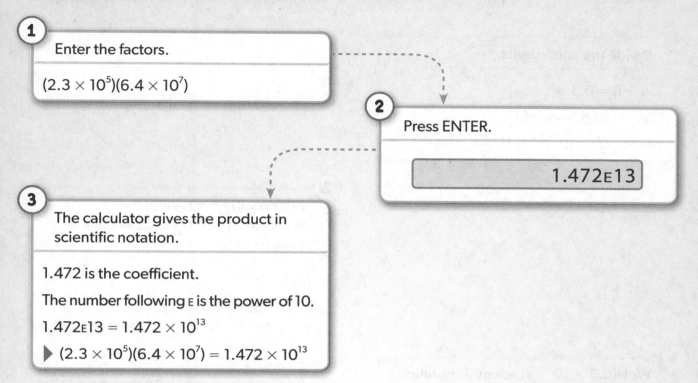

1 Enter the factors.

$(2.3 \times 10^5)(6.4 \times 10^7)$

2 Press ENTER.

1.472ᴇ13

3 The calculator gives the product in scientific notation.

1.472 is the coefficient.

The number following ᴇ is the power of 10.

$1.472\text{ᴇ}13 = 1.472 \times 10^{13}$

▶ $(2.3 \times 10^5)(6.4 \times 10^7) = 1.472 \times 10^{13}$

EXAMPLE D Verify the product found in Example C by using a calculator to multiply the numbers in standard form.

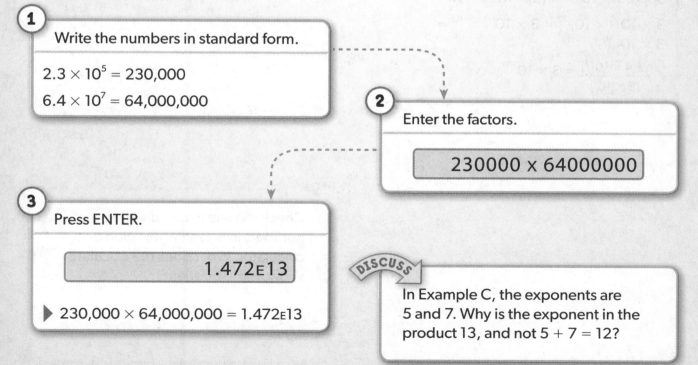

1 Write the numbers in standard form.

$2.3 \times 10^5 = 230{,}000$
$6.4 \times 10^7 = 64{,}000{,}000$

2 Enter the factors.

230000 x 64000000

3 Press ENTER.

1.472ᴇ13

▶ $230{,}000 \times 64{,}000{,}000 = 1.472\text{ᴇ}13$

DISCUSS

In Example C, the exponents are 5 and 7. Why is the exponent in the product 13, and not $5 + 7 = 12$?

EXAMPLE E Divide: $\dfrac{2.4 \times 10^{-4}}{8 \times 10^{6}}$. Express the quotient in scientific notation.

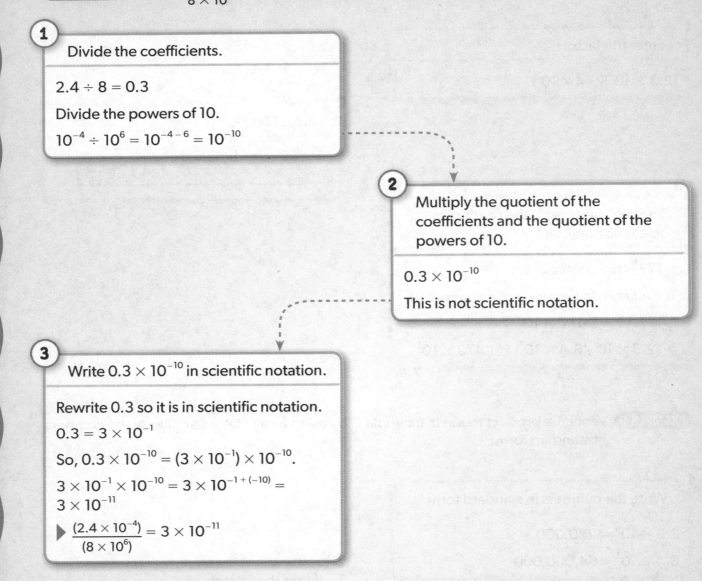

1 Divide the coefficients.

$2.4 \div 8 = 0.3$

Divide the powers of 10.

$10^{-4} \div 10^{6} = 10^{-4-6} = 10^{-10}$

2 Multiply the quotient of the coefficients and the quotient of the powers of 10.

0.3×10^{-10}

This is not scientific notation.

3 Write 0.3×10^{-10} in scientific notation.

Rewrite 0.3 so it is in scientific notation.

$0.3 = 3 \times 10^{-1}$

So, $0.3 \times 10^{-10} = (3 \times 10^{-1}) \times 10^{-10}$.

$3 \times 10^{-1} \times 10^{-10} = 3 \times 10^{-1 + (-10)} = 3 \times 10^{-11}$

▶ $\dfrac{(2.4 \times 10^{-4})}{(8 \times 10^{6})} = 3 \times 10^{-11}$

CHECK Check the answer by dividing the numbers in scientific notation on a calculator. What does the calculator show as the quotient?

⚙ Problem Solving

READ

A spacecraft leaves Earth's orbit at a speed of 7×10^5 km per day. To travel from Earth to Saturn, the craft needs to travel a total distance of 1.4×10^9 km. How long will it take the spacecraft to reach Saturn?

PLAN

Write an equation to represent the problem.

To find the time to reach Saturn, divide the distance the craft needs to travel by the speed of the craft.

Let n equal the number of days.

(_____) ÷ (_____) = n

SOLVE

Divide the coefficients: $1.4 \div 7 =$ _____.

Divide the powers of 10: $10^9 \div 10^5 =$ _____.

Set the quotient of the coefficients and the quotient of the powers of 10 as factors.

_____ $\times 10$ ‾‾‾

Write the expression in scientific notation.

_____ $\times 10$ ‾‾‾

Solve for n.

$n =$ _____

CHECK

Convert each number in scientific notation into standard form. Then divide using a calculator.

$7 \times 10^5 =$ _____

$1.4 \times 10^9 =$ _____

Perform the calculations on your calculator.

The calculator shows _____.

Does this match your answer? _____

▶ It will take _____ days for the spacecraft to reach Saturn.

Practice

Express each product in scientific notation.

1. $(4 \times 10^3)(2 \times 10^2)$

2. $(1 \times 10^5)(7 \times 10^9)$

3. $(5 \times 10^3)(3 \times 10^2)$

HINT

If the product of the coefficients is 10 or greater, what do you need to do to change it to scientific notation?

4. $(5.5 \times 10^4)(3 \times 10^{-2})$

5. $(3.2 \times 10^{-1})(4.5 \times 10^{-6})$

6. $(8.8 \times 10^{-5})(9.9 \times 10^6)$

Express each product in scientific notation and in standard form.

7. $(2 \times 10^4)(8 \times 10^{-3})$

8. $(4 \times 10^{-7})(7.5 \times 10^5)$

9. $(6.5 \times 10^8)(4.4 \times 10^{-6})$

Express each quotient in scientific notation.

10. $\dfrac{8 \times 10^8}{5 \times 10^5}$

11. $(5 \times 10^{-5}) \div (4 \times 10^6)$

12. $(1.2 \times 10^5) \div (5 \times 10^{-2})$

Express each quotient in scientific notation and in standard form.

13. $(9 \times 10^{-4}) \div (3 \times 10^{-5})$

14. $\dfrac{3.6 \times 10^8}{2.4 \times 10^6}$

15. $(8.4 \times 10^3) \div (2 \times 10^{-2})$

Express each product or quotient in scientific notation. Then check your answer with your calculator, explaining the calculator display.

16. $(2.5 \times 10^8)(1.2 \times 10^7)$

_____

_____

17. $(9.1 \times 10^{-3})(1.9 \times 10^{-8})$

_____

_____

18. $(8.25 \times 10^8) \div (1.5 \times 10^{-2})$

_____

_____

19. $(1.1 \times 10^{-5}) \div (5.5 \times 10^{11})$

_____

_____

Choose the best answer.

20. Momentum can be calculated by multiplying mass and speed. Which is the momentum of an object with a mass of 3.3×10^4 kg traveling at a speed of 3.2×10^3 m/s?

   A. 1.056×10^7 kg · m/s

   B. 1.56×10^7 kg · m/s

   C. 1.056×10^8 kg · m/s

   D. 1.56×10^8 kg · m/s

21. A computer can perform 4.5×10^2 instructions in a second. Which expression shows how long it would take to perform 1.8×10^{10} instructions?

   A. 4×10^5 seconds

   B. 4×10^7 seconds

   C. 4×10^8 seconds

   D. 8.1×10^{12} seconds

22. WRITE MATH Salvador estimates that there are about 1.5×10^4 grains of sand in a cubic centimeter of sand. He then estimates that there are about 7×10^{17} cubic centimeters of beach sand in the world. Explain the steps you would take to find how many grains of beach sand there are in the world.

_____

_____

23. DEMONSTRATE Experiment with your calculator to see when very small or very large numbers are converted to scientific notation. Why do you think the calculator is programmed to change the format for numbers at that size?

_____

_____

_____

Representing and Interpreting Proportional Relationships

UNDERSTAND A proportional relationship can be represented in different ways.

A right whale eats an average of 2 tons of plankton every day. The relationship between the number of days and the number of tons of plankton eaten can be expressed in a table.

Number of Days, x	Amount of Food Eaten (in tons), y
1	2
2	4
3	6
4	8
5	10

+1 { (between rows 1→2, 2→3, 3→4, 4→5)   } +2 (for each corresponding y change)

The ratio of the y-value to the x-value will always be 2:1. Similarly, the y-value always changes by the same amount (+2) when the x-value changes by the same amount (+1). Therefore, the relationship is proportional.

Another way to represent the proportional relationship in the table is with an equation. All proportional relationships have the form $y = kx$, where k is any nonzero number.

$$y = 2x$$

You can also represent a proportional relationship with a graph, as shown at the right. Using the x- and y-values from the table as ordered pairs or using the equation, you can plot the points on a coordinate plane and draw a straight line through the points. The graph of a proportional relationship always passes through point (0, 0), the **origin**.

The **slope** of a line is a ratio that compares the change in y-coordinates (the rise) of a graph to the change in x-coordinates (the run). In the line graphed at the right, the y-coordinates increase by 2 as the x-coordinates increase by 1, so the slope is $\frac{2}{1}$, or 2.

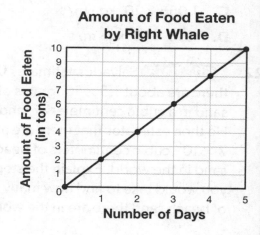

Amount of Food Eaten by Right Whale

⊏ Connect

The following graph represents the distance a car can travel based on the number of gallons of gas. The relationship is proportional.

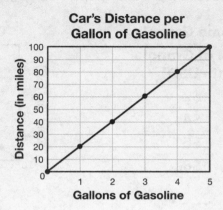

Car's Distance per Gallon of Gasoline

Find the miles per gallon, or **unit rate**, for the car.

1

Find the graph's rate of change to determine the unit rate.

The **rate of change** can be found by determining the slope. Choose any two points, (x_1, y_1) and (x_2, y_2), on the graph and write the ratio.

$$\frac{\text{change in } y\text{-values}}{\text{change in } x\text{-values}} = \frac{y_2 - y_1}{x_2 - x_1}$$

2

Substitute $(2, 40)$ for (x_1, y_1) and $(4, 80)$ for (x_2, y_2).

$$\frac{\text{change in } y\text{-values}}{\text{change in } x\text{-values}} = \frac{y_2 - y_1}{x_2 - x_1} = \frac{80 - 40}{4 - 2} = \frac{40}{2}$$

3

Simplify the fraction so that the denominator is 1. The resulting fraction will be the unit rate.

$$\frac{40}{2} = \frac{20}{1}$$

The unit rate represents the number of miles per 1 gallon.

▶ The unit rate is $\frac{20 \text{ miles}}{1 \text{ gallon}}$, or 20 mi/gal.

TRY

Compute the unit rate using two different points from the line. What do you notice?

EXAMPLE A A grocery store sells two varieties of trail mix: Wholesome Granola and Granolarama. Look at the table and graph.

Cost of Wholesome Granola

Ounces of Granola	Cost of Granola (in USD)
5	$2
10	$4
15	$6
20	$8

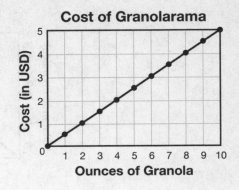

Cost of Granolarama

Which granola is the better buy?

1

Compare the unit rates.

The unit rate is the price of granola for 1 ounce. The better buy will be the granola with the lower unit rate.

2

Determine the unit rate of Wholesome Granola from the table.

To find the unit cost, divide the cost by the number of ounces.

$2 ÷ 5 oz = $0.40 per ounce

$4 ÷ 10 oz = $0.40 per ounce

$6 ÷ 15 oz = $0.40 per ounce

$8 ÷ 20 oz = $0.40 per ounce

The unit rate of Wholesome Granola is $0.40 per ounce.

3

Determine the unit rate of Granolarama from the graph.

Compare the change in y-coordinates (the rise) to the change in x-coordinates (the run). The line passes through (0, 0) and (10, 5).

$$\frac{\text{change in } y\text{-values}}{\text{change in } x\text{-values}} = \frac{5 - 0}{10 - 0} = \frac{5}{10} = 0.5$$

The unit rate of Granolarama is $0.50 per ounce.

4

Compare the unit rates.

$0.40 < 0.50$

▶ Wholesome Granola costs less than Granolarama per ounce. Wholesome Granola is the better buy.

MODEL

Write an equation to represent the information for each kind of granola.

EXAMPLE B Gus's Gaseteria sells gasoline using the following equation, where C is the total cost and g is the number of gallons of gasoline.

$$C = 3.35g$$

Sally's Station uses the following table to determine the total cost for buying different numbers of gallons of gasoline.

Cost of Gasoline at Sally's Station

Gallons of Gasoline	Cost of Gasoline (in USD)
2	$7
4	$14
6	$21
8	$28
10	$35

Which gas station's gasoline is the better buy?

1

Determine the slope from the Gus's Gaseteria equation.

An equation in the form "$y =$ " shows the slope as the coefficient of the x-value. It does not matter if different letters are used for the variables.

$$C = 3.35g$$

The slope of Gus's Gaseteria's equation is 3.35, so Gus's Gaseteria charges $3.35 per gallon.

2

Determine the slope from the Sally's Station table.

Use the first column of the table for the x-values and the second column for the y-values. For example, two ordered pairs would be (4, 14) and (8, 28).

$$\frac{\text{change in } y\text{-values}}{\text{change in } x\text{-values}} = \frac{28 - 14}{8 - 4} = \frac{14}{4} = 3.50$$

The slope from Sally's Station's table is 3.50, so Sally's Station charges $3.50 per gallon.

3

Compare the slopes.

$3.35 < 3.50$

▶ Gus's Gaseteria charges less than Sally's Station for 1 gallon of gasoline. Gasoline from Gus's Gaseteria is the better buy.

TRY

Terry charges $50 for 4 hours of tutoring. If this relationship between hours and charges were graphed, what would be the slope of the line?

Practice

Find each unit rate.

1. A bakery sells muffins using the equation $C = 1.85m$, where C is the cost of the muffins and m is the number of muffins.

   Unit rate = _____ per muffin

> **REMEMBER** An equation in the form "$y =$ " shows the unit rate in the coefficient of x.

2. **Cost of Croissants**

Number of Croissants	Cost
2	$3.50
4	$7.00
6	$10.50
8	$14.00

   Unit rate = _____ per croissant

3. **Cost of Bagels**

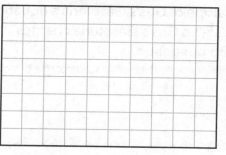

   Unit rate = _____ per bagel

Graph the proportional relationship. Then find the unit rate.

4. A grocer uses the following table to show the cost of different numbers of lemons.

Cost of Lemons

Number of Lemons	Cost (in USD)
3	$1
6	$2
9	$3
12	$4

   Unit rate = _____ per lemon

Cost of Lemons

Find each slope.

5. A farmer charges for his coffee beans using the equation $C = 3.95p$, where C is the cost of the coffee beans and p is the number of pounds of coffee beans.

Slope = _____

6.
Cost of Scarves

Number of Scarves	Cost (in USD)
4	$22.00
8	$44.00
12	$66.00
16	$88.00

Slope = _____

7.
Height of Stacked Boxes

Slope = _____

Solve.

8. **COMPARE** The maximum distance traveled by the space shuttle can be determined using the equation $d = 4.8s$, where d is the distance, in miles, and s is the number of seconds. The table below shows the distance traveled by the Apollo 10 astronauts returning from the moon.

Distance Traveled by Apollo 10

Number of Seconds	Distance Traveled (in miles)
5	23.5
10	47
15	70.5
20	94

Compare the slopes to determine which craft—the space shuttle or Apollo 10—traveled at a greater speed, and explain the steps you took.

_____

_____

_____

Relating Slope and *y*-intercept to Linear Equations

UNDERSTAND The slope of a line is the ratio of the line's vertical change, called the rise, to its horizontal change, called the run.

You can find the slope of a line from any two points on the line. You can confirm this by comparing the slopes of two segments on a line.

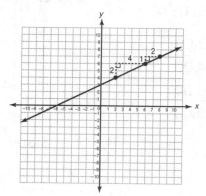

The slope, *m*, compares the change in *y*-values to the change in *x*-values. Use the points (2, 4) and (6, 6) to determine the slope.

$$m = \frac{\text{change in } y}{\text{change in } x}$$

$$= \frac{y_2 - y_1}{x_2 - x_1}$$

$$= \frac{6 - 4}{6 - 2} = \frac{2}{4} = \frac{1}{2}$$

$m = \frac{1}{2}$, so the slope of the line from (2, 4) to (6, 6) is $\frac{1}{2}$.

Use the points (6, 6) and (8, 7) to determine the slope.

$$m = \frac{\text{change in } y}{\text{change in } x}$$

$$= \frac{y_2 - y_1}{x_2 - x_1}$$

$$= \frac{7 - 6}{8 - 6} = \frac{1}{2}$$

$m = \frac{1}{2}$, so the slope of the line from (6, 6) to (8, 7) is $\frac{1}{2}$.

Compare the slopes.

$$\frac{1}{2} = \frac{1}{2}$$

The slope calculated from the first line segment is the same as the slope calculated from the second line segment. It does not matter which points on a line are used to determine slope.

⊏Connect

You can determine the equation of any line passing through the origin.

Determine the slope for the following line, which passes through the origin. Then use it to write the equation of the line.

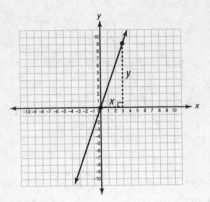

1 Use the given changes in *x* and *y* to determine the slope, *m*.

The change in *x* is labeled *x* on the graph.

The change in *y* is labeled *y* on the graph.

$$m = \frac{\text{change in } y \text{ values}}{\text{change in } x \text{ values}} = \frac{y}{x}$$

2 Solve the equation for *y*.

$$m = \frac{y}{x}$$

$$m(x) = \frac{y(x)}{x} \quad \leftarrow \text{ Multiply both sides by } x.$$

$$mx = y \quad \leftarrow \text{ Cancel the } x\text{'s on the right side.}$$

The equation is $y = mx$. This is the equation of any line that passes through the origin.

3 Use two points on the graph to find the slope, *m*.

The line passes through points (0, 0) and (3, 9).

$$m = \frac{y_2 - y_1}{x_2 - x_1} = \frac{9 - 0}{3 - 0} = \frac{9}{3} = 3$$

▶ The slope of the line that passes through (0, 0) and (3, 9) is 3. Using the equation $y = mx$, the equation of this line is $y = 3x$.

DISCUSS

If you know that a line passes through the origin and you know the coordinates of another point on the line, how can you use the equation $y = mx$ to determine the slope?

EXAMPLE What is the equation of the line graphed below?

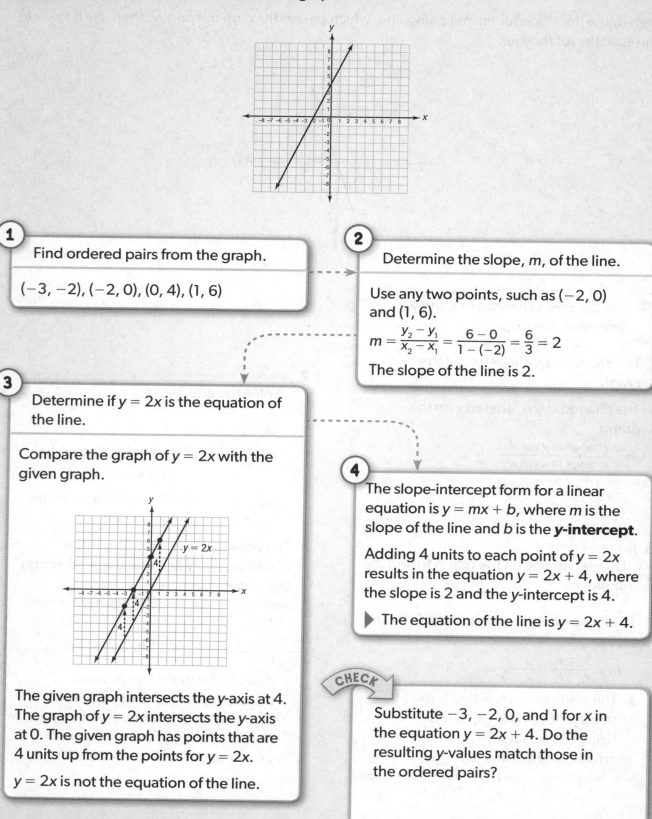

1 Find ordered pairs from the graph.

$(-3, -2)$, $(-2, 0)$, $(0, 4)$, $(1, 6)$

2 Determine the slope, m, of the line.

Use any two points, such as $(-2, 0)$ and $(1, 6)$.

$$m = \frac{y_2 - y_1}{x_2 - x_1} = \frac{6 - 0}{1 - (-2)} = \frac{6}{3} = 2$$

The slope of the line is 2.

3 Determine if $y = 2x$ is the equation of the line.

Compare the graph of $y = 2x$ with the given graph.

The given graph intersects the y-axis at 4. The graph of $y = 2x$ intersects the y-axis at 0. The given graph has points that are 4 units up from the points for $y = 2x$.

$y = 2x$ is not the equation of the line.

4 The slope-intercept form for a linear equation is $y = mx + b$, where m is the slope of the line and b is the **y-intercept**.

Adding 4 units to each point of $y = 2x$ results in the equation $y = 2x + 4$, where the slope is 2 and the y-intercept is 4.

▶ The equation of the line is $y = 2x + 4$.

CHECK

Substitute -3, -2, 0, and 1 for x in the equation $y = 2x + 4$. Do the resulting y-values match those in the ordered pairs?

Problem Solving

READ

A coordinate graph has points at (2, 4), (4, 6), and (8, 8). Can the points lie on the same line on the graph?

PLAN

Every line segment of a line has the same _____.

Therefore, if the _____ of the segment between (2, 4) and (4, 6) is the same as the _____ of the segment between (4, 6) and (8, 8), the points lie on the same line. If the _____ is not the same, then the points do not lie on the same line.

SOLVE

Find the _____ of the segment between (2, 4) and (4, 6).

$$\frac{y_2 - y_1}{x_2 - x_1} = \frac{\Box - \Box}{\Box - \Box} = \frac{\Box}{\Box} = \rule{2cm}{0.4pt}$$

Find the _____ of the segment between (4, 6) and (8, 8).

$$\frac{y_2 - y_1}{x_2 - x_1} = \frac{\Box - \Box}{\Box - \Box} = \frac{\Box}{\Box} = \rule{2cm}{0.4pt}$$

Therefore, the points (2, 4), (4, 6), and (8, 8) [do / do not] lie on the same line.

Circle one

CHECK

Use a coordinate graph to check the answer. Plot the given points on the graph.

The points (2, 4), (4, 6), and (8, 8) [do / do not] lie on the same line.

Does this match your answer? _____

▶ The points (2, 4), (4, 6), and (8, 8) [do / do not] lie on the same line.

Practice

Determine the slope and *y*-intercept from each graph.

1.

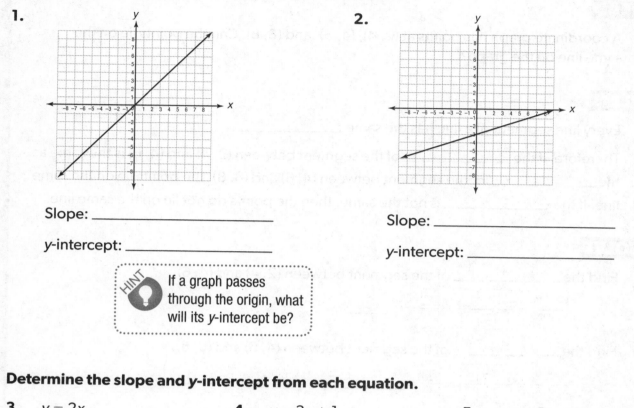

Slope: _____

y-intercept: _____

2.

Slope: _____

y-intercept: _____

HINT
If a graph passes through the origin, what will its *y*-intercept be?

Determine the slope and *y*-intercept from each equation.

3. $y = 2x$

Slope: _____

y-intercept: _____

4. $y = 3x + 1$

Slope: _____

y-intercept: _____

5. $y = -5x - 5$

Slope: _____

y-intercept: _____

6. $y = \frac{1}{2}x - 4$

Slope: _____

y-intercept: _____

7. $y = 1.25x + 8$

Slope: _____

y-intercept: _____

8. $y = -\frac{2}{3}x - 4.3$

Slope: _____

y-intercept: _____

Write an equation from each *y*-intercept and slope.

9. Slope: 1

y-intercept: 6

equation: _____

10. Slope: −3

y-intercept: −2

equation: _____

Determine the slope and y-intercept from each table of coordinates. Then write an equation and explain how you found the information to determine the equation.

11.

x	y
0	-7
2	-3
4	1
6	5

Slope: _____

y-intercept: _____

Equation: _____

_____

_____

12.

x	y
3	3
6	2
9	1
12	0

Slope: _____

y-intercept: _____

Equation: _____

_____

_____

Choose the best answer.

13. Which ordered pair represents a point that would lie on the graph of $y = 4x - 10$?

   A. $(4, -10)$

   B. $(4, 6)$

   C. $(-4, 6)$

   D. $(-4, 10)$

14. Which is the equation of a line that intersects the y-axis at 2 and has a slope of -2?

   A. $y = 2x - 2$

   B. $y = -2 + 2$

   C. $2y = -2x + 2$

   D. $y = -2x + 2$

Solve.

15. CONSTRUCT Write the equation of a line that passes through points $(4, 3)$ and $(8, 2)$. Describe the steps you took to form the equation.

_____

_____

_____

16. EXPLAIN In your own words, explain how you could tell whether $(-5, 2)$, $(-1, 0)$, and $(3, -2)$ lie in the same line.

_____

_____

_____

Solving Linear Equations in One Variable

UNDERSTAND To solve a linear equation in one variable, simplify the equation. Sometimes you may have to use the distributive property and combine like terms. Then isolate the variable on one side of the equation and solve for the variable. The resulting equation will tell you whether there is one solution, no solutions, or infinitely many solutions.

Solve: $4(x + 2) - 2x = 4x - 2$

Apply the distributive property.

$$4(x + 2) - 2x = 4x - 2$$
$$(4 \cdot x) + (4 \cdot 2) - 2x = 4x - 2$$
$$4x + 8 - 2x = 4x - 2$$

Combine like terms.

$$4x + 8 - 2x = 4x - 2 \quad \leftarrow \quad 4x \text{ and } -2x \text{ are like terms.}$$
$$2x + 8 = 4x - 2$$

Apply properties of equality so that the variable is on just one side of the equation.

$$2x + 8 = 4x - 2 \quad \leftarrow \quad \text{Subtract } 2x \text{ from both sides to remove } x \text{ from the left side.}$$
$$2x - 2x + 8 = 4x - 2 - 2x$$
$$8 = 2x - 2$$

Apply properties of equality to solve for x.

$$8 = 2x - 2$$
$$10 = 2x$$
$$10 \div 2 = 2x \div 2$$
$$5 = x$$

Check the solution by substituting into the original equation.

$$4(x + 2) - 2x = 4x - 2$$
$$4(\mathbf{5} + 2) - 2(\mathbf{5}) \stackrel{?}{=} 4(\mathbf{5}) - 2$$
$$4(7) - 2(5) \stackrel{?}{=} 4(5) - 2$$
$$4(7) - 10 \stackrel{?}{=} 20 - 2$$
$$28 - 10 \stackrel{?}{=} 18$$
$$18 = 18 \quad \checkmark \quad \text{The solution checks.}$$

← Connect

Solve: $5(2x - 4) = 3(3x - 6) + x - 2$

1

Apply the distributive property and combine like terms.

$$5(2x - 4) = 3(3x - 6) + x - 2$$

$$(5 \cdot 2x) + (5 \cdot -4) = (3 \cdot 3x) + (3 \cdot -6) + x - 2$$

$$10x - 20 = 9x - 18 + x - 2$$

$$10x - 20 = 10x - 20$$

2

Apply properties of equality to solve for x.

$$10x - 20 = 10x - 20$$

$$10x - 20 + 20 = 10x - 20 + 20$$

$$10x = 10x$$

$$\frac{10x}{10} = \frac{10x}{10}$$

$$x = x$$

The equation is true for all values of x. If you substitute any value for x in the original equation, it will result in a true statement.

▶ There are infinitely many solutions.

Solve: $2(x + 4) + 3 = 2x + 6$

1

Apply the distributive property and combine like terms.

$$2(x + 4) + 3 = 2x + 6$$

$$(2 \cdot x) + (2 \cdot 4) + 3 = 2x + 6$$

$$2x + 8 + 3 = 2x + 6$$

$$2x + 11 = 2x + 6$$

2

Apply properties of equality.

$$2x + 11 = 2x + 6$$

$$2x - 2x + 11 = 2x - 2x + 6$$

$$11 = 6$$

The equation results in a false statement. $11 \neq 6$. If you substitute any value for x in the original equation, it will give a false statement.

▶ There are no solutions for x.

MODEL

Write an equation that has infinitely many solutions and an equation that has no solution. What must be true about the variable terms on each side of the equations?

Practice

Solve each equation for *x*.

1. $3x + 1 = 4x - 2$

    $x = $ _____

2. $5(x - 6) - 2 = 2x - 5$

    $x = $ _____

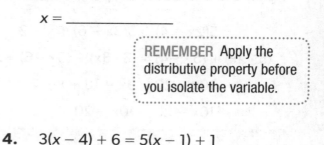

REMEMBER Apply the distributive property before you isolate the variable.

3. $7x + 12 = 2(x + 6)$

    $x = $ _____

4. $3(x - 4) + 6 = 5(x - 1) + 1$

    $x = $ _____

Solve each equation for *x*. If there are infinitely many solutions, write "infinitely many solutions." If there is no solution, write "no solution."

5. $3(x + 4) - 2 = 2(2x + 5) - x$

    _____

6. $2x + 1 - 3x + 5 = 3(x + 10)$

    _____

7. $3(x - 2) + 1 = 2(x - 4) + x + 13$

    _____

8. $0.1(5x + 20) - 5 = 0.25(2x + 8)$

    _____

9. $4(2.5x - 2) = 2(5x - 5) + 2$

    _____

10. $\frac{1}{2}(x - 6) + 1 = 2(x - 10) - 3$

    _____

Complete the steps to solve each equation.

11. $2\left(\frac{1}{3}x + 4\right) - 1 = \frac{4}{3}x - 3 + x$

Apply the distributive property: _____

_____

Combine like terms: _____

_____

Isolate and solve for x: _____

_____

Check your answer: _____

12. $4.5(x - 2) + 1.5x = 2(3x - 4) - 1$

Apply the distributive property: _____

_____

Combine like terms: _____

_____

Isolate and solve for x: _____

_____

Interpret the answer: _____

Choose the best answer.

13. What is the solution to the following?

$$4(x - 1) - 3x = -2x - 4 + 3x$$

A. $x = -4$

B. $x = 0$

C. no solution

D. infinite solutions

14. Which equation has exactly one solution?

A. $\frac{1}{5}x + 13 + x = -\frac{1}{10}(x + 40) + 4$

B. $4x - 4 + x = 2(3x - 2) - x$

C. $2(4x + 5) - 10 = 4(2x - 3) + 12$

D. $2.5(2x - 4) = 4(x - 4) + x$

Solve.

15. EXPLAIN If an equation in one variable contains a variable term on both sides of the equals sign, explain what steps you need to take to solve for the variable.

_____

_____

_____

16. EXPLAIN In your own words, explain what it means when a solution to an equation in one variable results in an inequality, such as $3 \neq 4$.

_____

_____

_____

Solving Systems of Two Linear Equations Graphically

UNDERSTAND You can find the solution of a system by graphing the two lines and identifying the coordinates of the point(s) of intersection. There may be no solution, one solution, or infinitely many solutions.

Find the solution(s) to $y = 2x - 3$ and $y = 2x + 2$.

Graph the equations.

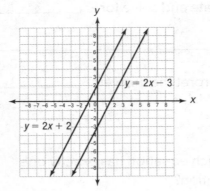

The lines do not intersect.

There is no solution.

Find the solution(s) to $y = 4x - 4$ and $y = x + 2$.

Graph the equations.

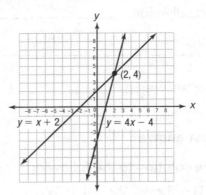

The lines intersect at (2, 4).

There is one solution, (2, 4).

Find the solution(s) to $y = -x + 1$ and $x + y = 1$.

Graph the equations.

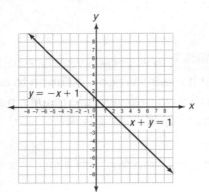

The lines are identical. They coincide. **Coincident lines** intersect at every point.

There are infinitely many solutions.

⊏ Connect

Find the solution(s) to $y = x + 3$ and $y = 2x - 2$.

1

Find some ordered pairs for $y = x + 3$.

Create a table of values. Use any values for x. Then substitute those x-values and find the resulting y-values.

$y = x + 3$

x	y
−3	0
−1	2
1	4
3	6
5	8

2

Find some ordered pairs for $y = 2x - 2$.

Create a table of values. Use any values for x. Then substitute those x-values and find the resulting y-values.

$y = 2x - 2$

x	y
−3	−8
−1	−4
1	0
3	4
5	8

3

Graph the system of equations.

Graph the ordered pairs for each equation and draw a line through each set of points.

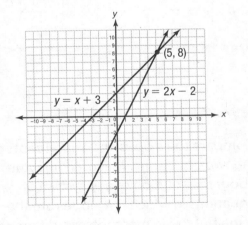

The one point of intersection is at (5, 8).

▶ The solution is (5, 8).

4

Check the solution.

Substitute 5 for x and 8 for y in both equations.

$y = x + 3$	$y = 2x - 2$
$8 \stackrel{?}{=} 5 + 3$	$8 \stackrel{?}{=} 2(5) - 2$
$8 = 8 ✓$	$8 \stackrel{?}{=} 10 - 2$
	$8 = 8 ✓$

The ordered pair (5, 8) satisfies both equations, so the solution is correct.

TRY

Find the solution(s) to the system $y = -x + 2$ and $y = 2x - 1$.

EXAMPLE A Find the solution(s) to $y = \frac{1}{2}x - 6$ and $y = \frac{1}{2}x$.

1

Find some ordered pairs for $y = \frac{1}{2}x - 6$.

Create a table of values for the equation. Use any values for x. Then find the resulting y-values.

$$y = \frac{1}{2}x - 6$$

x	y
−4	−8
−2	−7
0	−6
2	−5
4	−4

2

Find some ordered pairs for $y = \frac{1}{2}x$.

Create a table of values for the equation. Use any values for x. Then find the resulting y-values.

$$y = \frac{1}{2}x$$

x	y
−4	−2
−2	−1
0	0
2	1
4	2

3

Graph the system of equations.

Graph the ordered pairs for each equation and draw a line through each set of points.

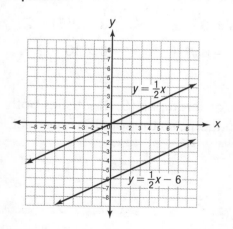

▶ There is no point of intersection. The system of equations has no solution.

DISCUSS

Compare the slopes and y-intercepts of the two equations. Make a conjecture about the solution of any system of equations in which the slopes are the same but the y-intercepts are different. How could you test your conjecture?

EXAMPLE B Find the solution(s) to $3x + y = 2$ and $6x + 2y = 4$.

1

Convert $3x + y = 2$ to slope-intercept form: $y = mx + b$.

$3x + y = 2$ ← Subtract 3x from each side.

$3x + y - 3x = 2 - 3x$

$y = -3x + 2$

2

Convert $6x + 2y = 4$ to slope-intercept form: $y = mx + b$.

$6x + 2y = 4$ ← Subtract 6x from each side.

$6x + 2y - 6x = 4 - 6x$

$2y = -6x + 4$ ← Divide both sides by 2.

$y = -3x + 2$

3

Compare the slopes and y-intercepts of the equations.

$y = -3x + 2$ slope = -3, y-intercept = 2

$y = -3x + 2$ slope = -3, y-intercept = 2

The equations are identical. Because the equations have the same slope and y-intercept, their graphs will intersect at every point.

▶ The lines coincide and have infinitely many solutions.

4

Check your answer.

You can graph the equations to check that they are coincident.

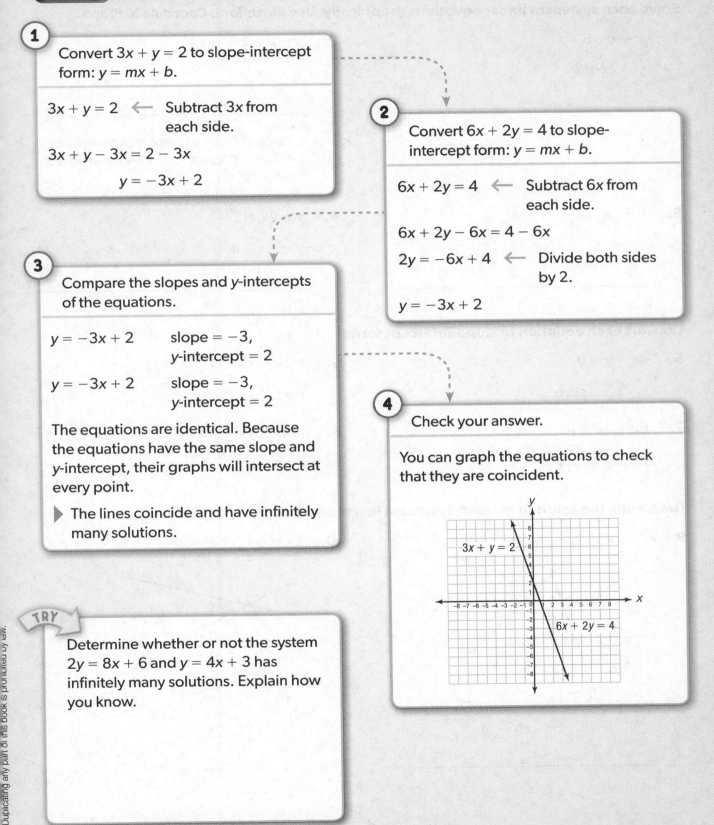

$3x + y = 2$

$6x + 2y = 4$

TRY

Determine whether or not the system $2y = 8x + 6$ and $y = 4x + 3$ has infinitely many solutions. Explain how you know.

Practice

Solve each system of linear equations graphically. Use *Math Tool: Coordinate Plane*.

1. $y = x + 6$

$y = 2x + 3$

_____

2. $y = x + 2$

$y = -x$

_____

> REMEMBER An equation in slope-intercept form that does not have a b-value intersects the y-axis at 0.

3. $y = \frac{1}{2}x - 4$

$y = x - 7$

_____

4. $y = 2x + 2$

$y = -x - 4$

_____

Convert each equation to slope-intercept form.

5. $4x + y = 0$

$y = $ _____

6. $-3x + y = -3$

$y = $ _____

7. $6x + 3y = 18$

$y = $ _____

8. $15x - 5y = -10$

$y = $ _____

Determine the solution for each system of linear equations.

9.

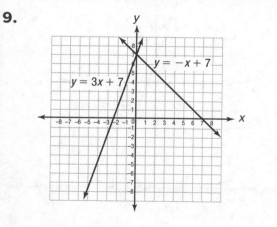

10.

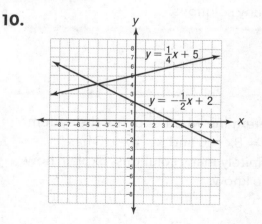

_____   _____

Solve each system of linear equations graphically. Use *Math Tool: Coordinate Plane*.

11. $y = \frac{3}{2}x + \frac{1}{2}$

    $y = \frac{3}{2}x - 4\frac{1}{2}$

    _____

12. $-2x + y = -5$

    $4x - 2y = 10$

    _____

13. $y = -2.5x - 6.5$

    $y = 0.5x - 9.5$

    _____

14. $y = \frac{1}{2}x - 5$

    $\frac{1}{5}x - y = 2$

    _____

15. $y = -4x + 1$

    $8x + 2y = 3$

    _____

16. $3x + y = 10$

    $-9x - 3y = -30$

    _____

Without graphing, determine whether each system of equations will have no solution, one solution, or infinitely many solutions. Explain your answer.

17. $y = \frac{3}{5}x + 2$

    $y = \frac{3}{5}x$

    _____

    _____

18. $y = 6x + 2$

    $-12x + 2y = 4$

    _____

    _____

Solve.

19. **APPLY** One day, a toy store sells 3 xylophones and 3 yo-yos for $33. Another day, it sells 2 xylophones and 1 yo-yo for $19. Equations that represent the sales for the two days are $3x + 3y = 33$ and $2x + y = 19$, where x is the number of xylophones sold and y is the number of yo-yos sold. Solve the system of equations graphically to determine the value of one xylophone and one yo-yo. Use *Math Tool: Coordinate Plane*, and explain your answer.

    _____

    _____

11 Solving Systems of Two Linear Equations Algebraically

EXAMPLE A Solve the system of equations algebraically: $3x - 2y = -1$ and $-x + 2y = -5$

1

Line up the equations vertically.

$3x - 2y = -1$

$-x + 2y = -5$

The y-coefficients are opposites: 2 and -2. Because they are opposites, their sum will equal 0.

2

Apply the addition property of equality.

Add the left sides of the equations by combining like terms.

Add the right sides of the equations by combining like terms.

$$3x - 2y = -1$$
$$\underline{+ \; -x + 2y = -5}$$
$$2x + 0y = -6$$

The term $0y$ is equal to 0. The sum of the equations is therefore $2x = -6$.

3

Solve for the variable.

$2x = -6$

$\dfrac{2x}{2} = -\dfrac{6}{2}$

$x = -3$

4

Use the value for one variable to find the value of the other. Do this by substituting the value found into one of the original equations.

$3x - 2y = -1$

$3(-3) - 2y = -1$

$-9 - 2y = -1$

$-9 - 2y + 9 = -1 + 9$

$-2y = 8$

$\dfrac{-2y}{-2} = -\dfrac{8}{2}$

$y = -4$

5

Use the x-value and y-value to form an ordered pair (x, y).

$x = -3$ and $y = -4$

▶ The solution is $(-3, -4)$.

CHECK

Substitute -3 for x and -4 for y in the original equations. Does the solution check?

EXAMPLE B Solve the system of equations: $2x + 4y = 2$ and $3x + 2y = 11$

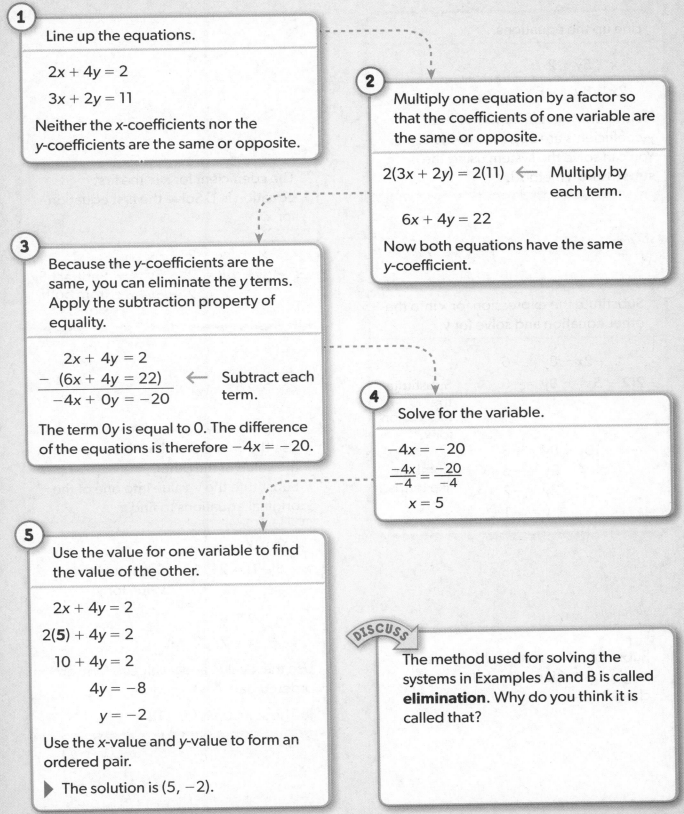

1

Line up the equations.

$2x + 4y = 2$

$3x + 2y = 11$

Neither the x-coefficients nor the y-coefficients are the same or opposite.

2

Multiply one equation by a factor so that the coefficients of one variable are the same or opposite.

$2(3x + 2y) = 2(11)$ ← Multiply by each term.

$6x + 4y = 22$

Now both equations have the same y-coefficient.

3

Because the y-coefficients are the same, you can eliminate the y terms. Apply the subtraction property of equality.

$$\begin{array}{r} 2x + 4y = 2 \\ - \ (6x + 4y = 22) \\ \hline -4x + 0y = -20 \end{array}$$ ← Subtract each term.

The term $0y$ is equal to 0. The difference of the equations is therefore $-4x = -20$.

4

Solve for the variable.

$-4x = -20$

$\dfrac{-4x}{-4} = \dfrac{-20}{-4}$

$x = 5$

5

Use the value for one variable to find the value of the other.

$2x + 4y = 2$

$2(\mathbf{5}) + 4y = 2$

$10 + 4y = 2$

$4y = -8$

$y = -2$

Use the x-value and y-value to form an ordered pair.

▶ The solution is $(5, -2)$.

DISCUSS

The method used for solving the systems in Examples A and B is called **elimination**. Why do you think it is called that?

EXAMPLE C Solve the system of equations: $x + 5y = 2$ and $-2x - 8y = -6$

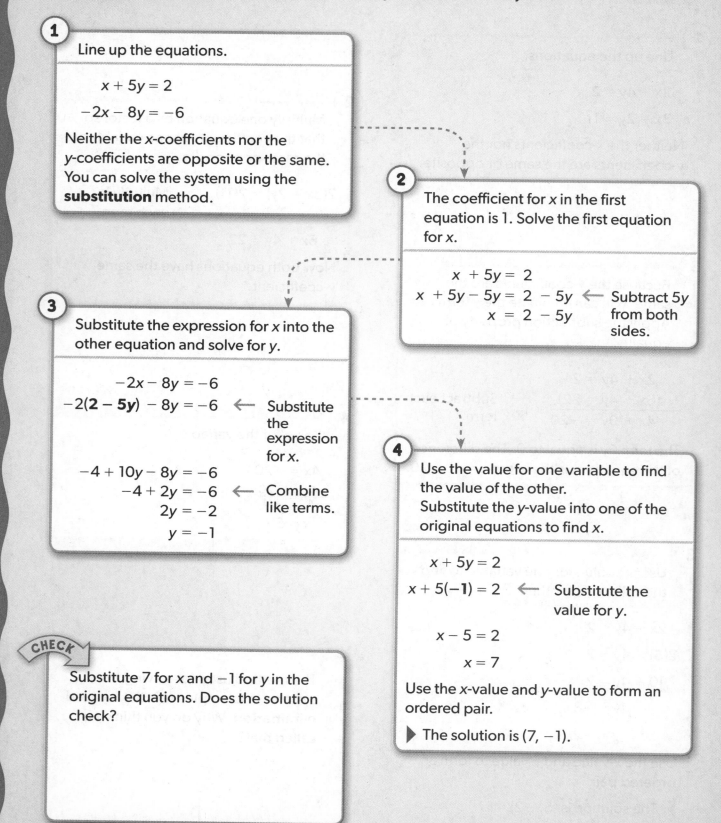

1

Line up the equations.

$$x + 5y = 2$$
$$-2x - 8y = -6$$

Neither the x-coefficients nor the y-coefficients are opposite or the same. You can solve the system using the **substitution** method.

2

The coefficient for x in the first equation is 1. Solve the first equation for x.

$$x + 5y = 2$$
$$x + 5y - 5y = 2 - 5y \quad \leftarrow \text{Subtract } 5y$$
$$x = 2 - 5y \qquad \text{from both sides.}$$

3

Substitute the expression for x into the other equation and solve for y.

$$-2x - 8y = -6$$
$$-2(\mathbf{2 - 5y}) - 8y = -6 \quad \leftarrow \text{Substitute the expression for } x.$$
$$-4 + 10y - 8y = -6$$
$$-4 + 2y = -6 \quad \leftarrow \text{Combine like terms.}$$
$$2y = -2$$
$$y = -1$$

4

Use the value for one variable to find the value of the other.
Substitute the y-value into one of the original equations to find x.

$$x + 5y = 2$$
$$x + 5(\mathbf{-1}) = 2 \quad \leftarrow \text{Substitute the value for } y.$$
$$x - 5 = 2$$
$$x = 7$$

Use the x-value and y-value to form an ordered pair.

▶ The solution is $(7, -1)$.

CHECK

Substitute 7 for x and -1 for y in the original equations. Does the solution check?

EXAMPLE D Solve the system of equations: $5x - y = -1$ and $-10x + 2y = -6$

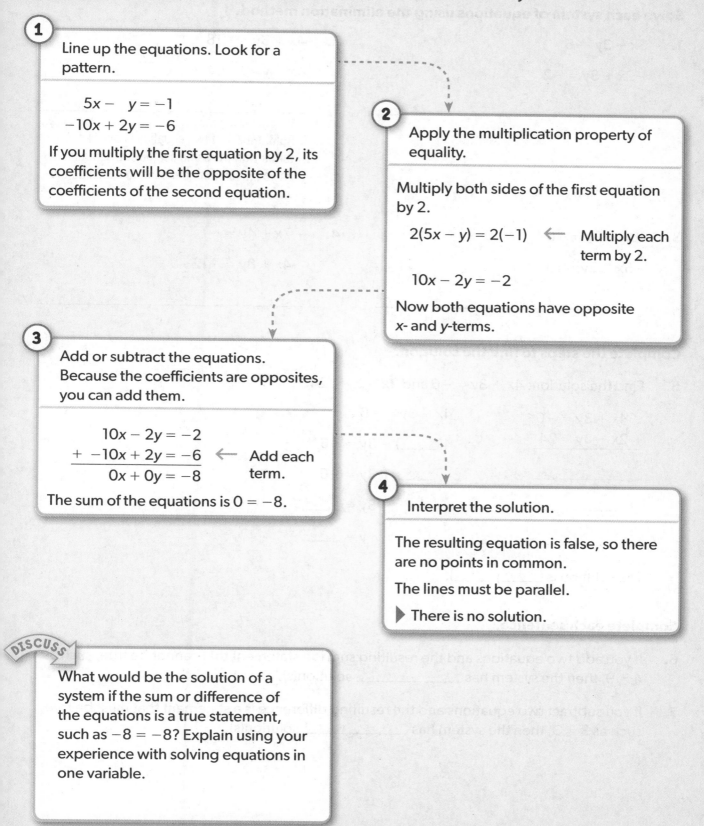

1 Line up the equations. Look for a pattern.

$$5x - y = -1$$
$$-10x + 2y = -6$$

If you multiply the first equation by 2, its coefficients will be the opposite of the coefficients of the second equation.

2 Apply the multiplication property of equality.

Multiply both sides of the first equation by 2.

$$2(5x - y) = 2(-1) \quad \leftarrow \text{Multiply each term by 2.}$$

$$10x - 2y = -2$$

Now both equations have opposite x- and y-terms.

3 Add or subtract the equations. Because the coefficients are opposites, you can add them.

$$10x - 2y = -2$$
$$+ \ -10x + 2y = -6 \quad \leftarrow \text{Add each term.}$$
$$\overline{0x + 0y = -8}$$

The sum of the equations is $0 = -8$.

4 Interpret the solution.

The resulting equation is false, so there are no points in common.

The lines must be parallel.

▶ There is no solution.

DISCUSS

What would be the solution of a system if the sum or difference of the equations is a true statement, such as $-8 = -8$? Explain using your experience with solving equations in one variable.

Practice

Solve each system of equations using the elimination method.

1. $3x - 3y = 6$

   $-2x + 3y = -2$

   _____

2. $4x + 3y = -18$

   $4x - y = -10$

   _____

> **REMEMBER** If two equations have like terms with the same coefficient, subtract one equation from the other to eliminate the variable.

3. $10x + 2y = -6$

   $-5x - 3y = 19$

   _____

4. $-7x + 4y = -1$

   $-4x + 8y = -12$

   _____

Complete the steps to find the solution.

5. Find the solution: $4x + 3y = -6$ and $2x - 3y = 24$.

   $4x + 3y = -6$
   $\underline{+\ 2x - 3y = 24}$

   _____

   $x = $ _____

   $4x + 3y = -6$

   $4(\underline{\quad}) + 3y = -6$

   $\underline{\quad} + 3y = -6$

   $3y = \underline{\quad}$

   $y = \underline{\quad}$

   The solution is (_____, _____).

Complete each sentence.

6. If you add two equations and the resulting sum is a statement that cannot be true, such as $4 = 9$, then the system has _____ solution(s).

7. If you subtract two equations and the resulting difference is a statement that must be true, such as $3 = 3$, then the system has _____ solution(s).

Solve each system of equations using substitution.

8. $x + 4y = -15$

$3x + 3y = 0$

_____

9. $9x - 8y = -6$

$x - 3y = -7$

_____

10. $6x - 5y = -3$

$-4x + y = -5$

_____

11. $12x + 2y = -4$

$-5x + y = 20$

_____

Match each system with its number of solutions.

12. $-4x + y = 2$

$8x - 2y = -4$

no solution

13. $3x - 4y = 0$

$7x + 4y = 0$

one solution

14. $x + y = -8$

$4x + 4y = -8$

infinitely many solutions

Solve.

15. (EXPLAIN) A system of equations consists of $3x + 7y = 8$ and $2x + 4y = 6$. Choose a method for finding the solution and explain how you would use it to find the solution.

_____

_____

_____

16. (PREDICT) Without solving graphically or algebraically, predict the solution for the following system of equations.

$5x - 2y = 8$
$5x - 2y = -8$

Explain how you can tell.

_____

_____

_____

12 Problem Solving: Using Systems of Equations

READ

Nina has $5 bills and $10 bills in her wallet. She has a total of 7 bills with a value of $55. How many of each type of bill does she have?

PLAN

Set up a system of equations to solve algebraically.

Let f equal the number of $5 bills in Nina's wallet and let t equal the number of $10 bills in Nina's wallet.

Write an equation to represent the number of bills in Nina's wallet.

_____ + _____ = 7

Write another equation to represent the value of the bills in Nina's wallet.

_____ + _____ = 55

SOLVE

Solve the system of equations using substitution.

Set the first equation equal to a variable.

$f + t = 7$, so $f = $ _____.

Substitute the expression equal to f into the other equation. Then solve for t.

5(_____) + _____ = 55

$t = $ _____

Substitute the value for t into either original equation to find the value of f.

_____ + _____ = _____

$f = $ _____

CHECK

Substitute the values for f and t back into your original equations.

Do the substitutions result in true equations? _____

▶ Nina has _____ $5 bills and _____ $10 bills in her wallet.

Ralph's Deli

READ

The cost of 3 pizzas and 4 sandwiches at Ralph's Deli is $68. The cost of 3 pizzas and 7 sandwiches is $92. What is the cost of one pizza and the cost of one sandwich?

PLAN

Set up a system of equations to solve algebraically.

Let p equal the cost of a _____ and let s equal the cost of a _____.

Write an equation to represent the cost of 3 pizzas and 4 sandwiches.

_____ + _____ = 68

Write another equation to represent the cost of 3 pizzas and 7 sandwiches.

_____ + _____ = 92

SOLVE

Solve the system of equations using elimination.

Stack the equations. Then add or subtract.

$$\underline{\hspace{2cm}} + \underline{\hspace{2cm}} = 68$$

$$+ \text{ or } - (\underline{\hspace{2cm}} + \underline{\hspace{2cm}} = 92)$$

$$\underline{\hspace{2cm}} + \underline{\hspace{2cm}} = \underline{\hspace{2cm}}$$

Rewrite the equation with only one variable. Then solve for the variable.

_____ $s =$ _____

$s =$ _____

Substitute the value for s into either original equation to find the value of p.

_____ + _____ = _____

$p =$ _____

CHECK

Substitute the values for p and s back into your original equations.

Do the substitutions result in true equations? _____

▶ The cost of a pizza is _____. The cost of a sandwich is _____.

Practice

Use the 4-step problem-solving process to solve each problem.

1. **READ**   The cost of 3 tacos and 1 juice is $7. The cost of 4 tacos and 2 juices is $10. If t = the cost of a taco and j = the cost of a juice, the scenario can be represented by the following system:

$$3t + j = 7$$
$$4t + 2j = 10$$

What is the cost of one taco and one juice?

PLAN _____

_____

SOLVE

CHECK

2.   There are 15 coins, which are nickels and dimes only, in Edith's purse. The total value of the coins in her purse is $1.15. If n = nickels and d = dimes, the scenario can be represented by the following system:

$$n + d = 15$$
$$0.05n + 0.10d = 1.15$$

How many nickels and dimes are in Edith's purse?

3. A warehouse stacks 3 identical large boxes and 2 identical small boxes to a height of 11 feet. It also stacks 2 large boxes and 1 small box to a height of 7 feet. What are the heights of a small box and a large box?

4. One day, an electronics store ships 4 identical laptop computers and 5 identical monitors, for a combined weight of 60 pounds. Another day, it ships 2 laptop computers and 4 monitors, for a combined weight of 42 pounds. What is the weight of one laptop and the weight of one monitor?

5. Kiana and Jacobi each have a collection of identical red marbles and identical blue marbles. Kiana's collection of 12 red marbles and 8 blue marbles has a mass of 70 grams. Jacobi's collection of 20 red marbles and 12 blue marbles has a mass of 110 grams. What is the mass of each color marble?

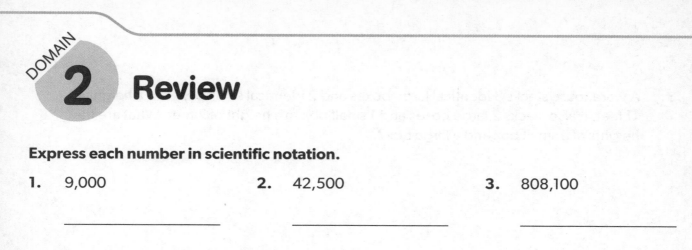

DOMAIN 2 Review

Express each number in scientific notation.

1. 9,000

2. 42,500

3. 808,100

_____

_____

_____

Graph the proportional relationship. Then use the slope of the line to find the unit rate.

4. A printer manufacturer uses the following table to show how long it takes to print different numbers of photographs.

Speed of Photo Printer

Number of Photos Printed	Time (in minutes)
4	2
8	4
12	6
16	8

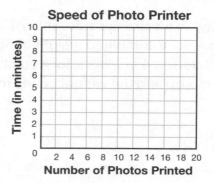

Unit rate = _____ per photograph

Choose the best answer.

5. What is the solution to the following?

$$x + 5 + x + 1 + x = 3(x + 2) + 1$$

   A. $x = 1$

   B. $x = 3$

   C. no solution

   D. infinitely many solutions

6. What is the solution to the following system of linear equations?

$$-4x + 2y = 10$$
$$2x - 2y = -10$$

   A. $(5, 0)$

   B. $(0, 5)$

   C. no solution

   D. infinitely many solutions

Express each product or quotient in scientific notation.

7. $(4.6 \times 10^3)(5.3 \times 10^2)$

_____

8. $\dfrac{1.6 \times 10^5}{8 \times 10^3}$

_____

Complete each sentence.

9. To evaluate $7^{-4} \times 7^4$, _____ the exponents. The answer in exponential form is _____. The answer in standard form is _____.

10. To evaluate $(3^5)^{-1}$, _____ the exponents. The answer in exponential form is _____. The answer in standard form is _____.

11. To evaluate $\frac{m^{-3}}{m^4}$, _____ the exponents. The answer in exponential form is _____.

Graph each system of equations to find its solution. Use *Math Tool: Coordinate Plane*.

12. $y = 2x - 2$
    $y = \frac{1}{2}x + 4$

    Solution = _____

13. $y = 2x - 1$
    $y = -3x - 11$

    Solution = _____

Choose the best answer.

14. What is the solution to the following?

    $$2\left(\frac{1}{5}x - 3\right) + x = 4\left(\frac{1}{4}x - \frac{1}{2}\right)$$

    A. $x = 4$

    B. $x = 10$

    C. no solution

    D. infinitely many solutions

15. Which is the principal square root of 121?

    A. -11

    B. 11

    C. ± 11

    D. $\pm\sqrt{121}$

Evaluate each expression. Leave your answer in exponential form.

16. $7^9 \times 7^5$

17. $4^{-2} \times 4^8$

18. $\frac{10^7}{10^4}$

Evaluate each expression. Write your answer in standard form.

19. $3^3 \times 3^2$

20. $\frac{5^6}{5^4}$

21. $\left(\frac{3}{11}\right)^2$

Find the cube root of each number.

22. $\sqrt[3]{64}$

_____

23. $\sqrt[3]{1}$

_____

24. $\sqrt[3]{216}$

_____

Solve for x.

25. $x^2 = 625$

_____

_____

26. $x^3 = -216$

_____

_____

27. $x^2 = \dfrac{25}{36}$

_____

_____

Solve.

28. All pairs of corresponding sides of two similar triangles have the same ratio. Use that information and the diagram at the right to show why any two segments on line AC have the same slope.

_____

_____

_____

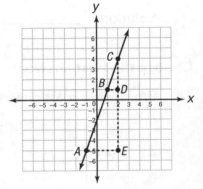

Use the situation below to answer questions 29 and 30.

A theater sells regularly priced tickets for $12 and discounted tickets for $8. On one afternoon, the total number of regularly priced tickets and discounted tickets sold was 60, and the total ticket sales came to $620.

29. **WRITE** Let r = the number of regularly priced tickets and d = the number of discounted tickets. Write a system of equations to represent this scenario.

_____

_____

30. **SHOW** Solve the system to determine how many of each type of ticket was sold. Show your work.

_____

_____

_____

Classroom Measurements

For this activity, you will take measurements in both customary and metric units. You will need a tape measure or yardstick with U.S. customary units and a tape measure or meter stick with metric units.

Use a tape measure to determine the length or height of several objects in the classroom. Express each length or height in scientific notation. Then use scientific notation to express the measurements as very small or very large numbers.

Object	Height/Length (in inches)	Height/Length (in inches) in Scientific Notation	Height/Length (in centimeters)	Height/Length (in centimeters) in Scientific Notation
Height of desk				
Length of classroom				
Height of student				
Length of desk				
Height of classroom				
_____				

There are 63,360 inches in a mile and 100,000 centimeters in a kilometer. Express each number in scientific notation.

_____   _____

There are 10 millimeters in a centimeter. There are 10,000 microns in a centimeter. Express each number in scientific notation.

_____   _____

Use your measurements and the unit conversions in scientific notation to complete the following table.

Object	Height/Length (in miles)	Height/Length (in km)	Height/Length (in mm)	Height/Length (in microns)
Height of desk				
Length of classroom				
Height of student				
Length of desk				
Height of classroom				
_____				

Grade 7

Grade 8

Grade 7 RP

Analyze proportional relationships and use them to solve real-world and mathematical problems.

Grade 7 NS

Apply and extend previous understandings of operations with fractions to add, subtract, multiply, and divide rational numbers.

Grade 8 F

Define, evaluate, and compare functions.

Use functions to model relationships between quantities.

Grade 7 EE

Solve real-life and mathematical problems using numerical and algebraic expressions and equations.

Domain 3
Functions

13 Introducing Functions

LESSON

UNDERSTAND A **relation** is a set of input values and output values, often written as ordered pairs. The first number in an ordered pair is the input value. The second number is the output value. A **function** is a rule that assigns to each input value *exactly one* output value.

Tell whether the relation {(2, 4), (4, 6), (2, 8), (6, 3)} represents a function.

The mapping below shows each input value and its corresponding output value.

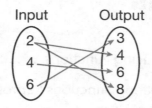

The input value 2 is assigned to two different output values: 4 and 8.
This relation is not a function.

Tell whether the relation {(3, 1), (5, 3), (2, 8), (6, 8)} represents a function.

Graph the ordered pairs.

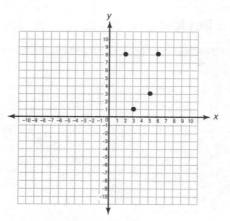

Each input value has exactly one output value.
This relation is a function.

⊸ Connect

The table below shows some ordered pairs for the equation $y = \pm\sqrt{x}$.
Determine whether the relation is a function.

x	9	4	1	0	1	4	9
y	−3	−2	−1	0	1	2	3

1 Graph the ordered pairs. Draw a curve through the points.

2 Draw some vertical lines through the graph to see if any input value has more than one corresponding output value.

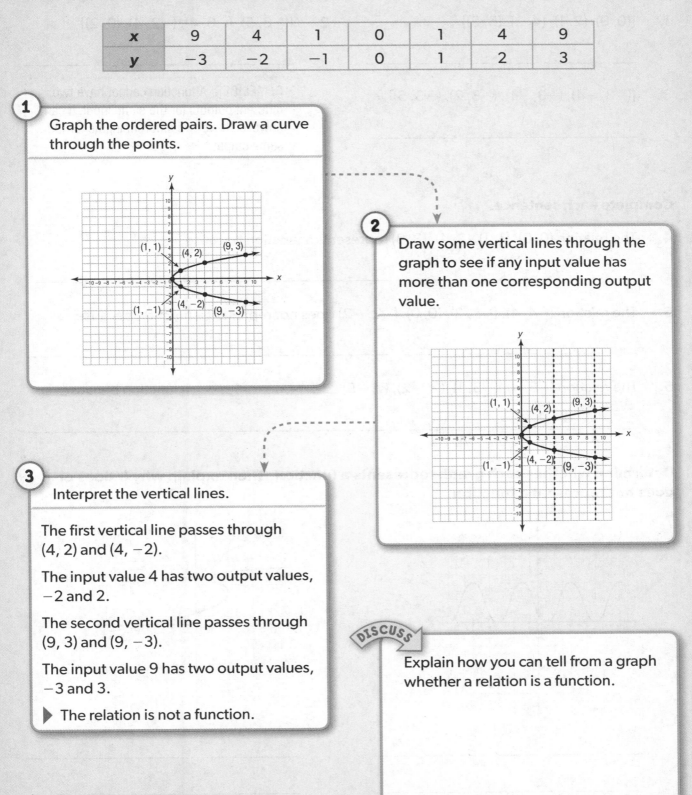

3 Interpret the vertical lines.

The first vertical line passes through (4, 2) and (4, −2).

The input value 4 has two output values, −2 and 2.

The second vertical line passes through (9, 3) and (9, −3).

The input value 9 has two output values, −3 and 3.

▶ The relation is not a function.

DISCUSS

Explain how you can tell from a graph whether a relation is a function.

Practice

Determine whether each set of ordered pairs represents a function.

1. {(0, 0), (2, 1), (4, 2), (6, 3)}

_____

2. {(−8, 5), (−6, 4), (−2, 4), (0, 2)}

_____

3. {(−3, −4), (−3, −1), (−3, 2), (−3, 5)}

_____

> **REMEMBER** A function cannot have two different outputs for the same input. It can, however, have two different inputs for the same output.

Complete each sentence.

4. The relation (0, 0), (1, 1), (2, 4), (3, 9) represents a function because

_____.

5. The relation (−4, 4), (−2, 2), (0, 0), (−2, −2) does not represent a function because

_____.

6. The relation (−8, 4), (−3, 1), (2, −2), (7, −5) _____ a function because

_____.

Determine whether each graph represents a function. Then explain why it does or does not represent a function.

7.

8.

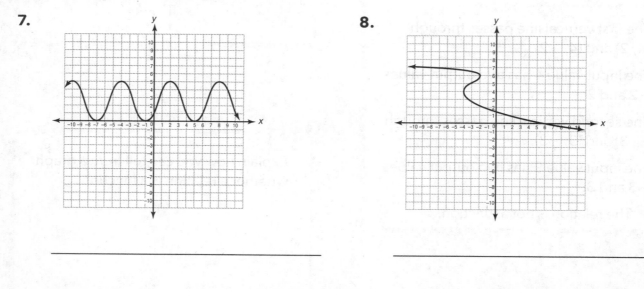

_____   _____

_____   _____

Graph each relation from its description or ordered pairs to determine whether it represents a function. Then explain why it does or does not represent a function.

9. Each output value is equal to the square of the input value minus 5.

10.

x	0	2	4	2	0	2	4
y	8	6	4	2	0	−2	−4

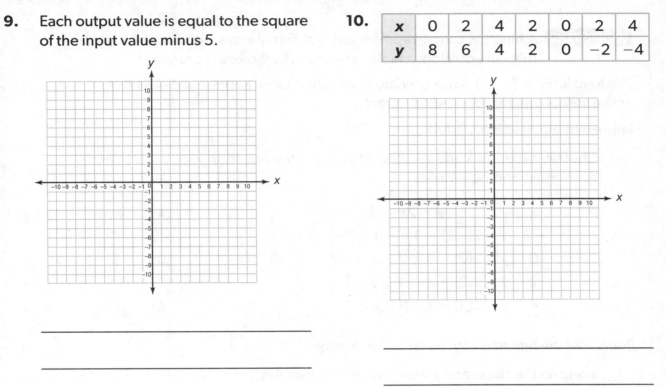

_____

_____

_____

_____

Solve.

11. **JUDGE** Yoshi draws a vertical line on the graph of a relation. His vertical line intersects only 1 point of the graph. He determines that the relation is also a function. Assess Yoshi's conclusion and explain why it is or is not necessarily correct.

_____

_____

_____

12. **DEDUCE** The graph of a linear equation is in the form $y = mx + b$. Are there any values of m that would result in the graph **not** representing a function? Explain your answer.

_____

_____

_____

LESSON 14
Comparing Functions Represented in Different Ways

UNDERSTAND A function can be represented in different ways. You can use a verbal rule, an equation, a table, or a graph to represent a function.

The function $y = 2x - 3$ is represented in equation form. Represent it in a table, with a verbal description, and as a graph.

Represent the function in a table.

Choose values for x and substitute them into the equation $y = 2x - 3$ to find the corresponding y-values.

x	$y = 2x - 3$	y
-2	$y = 2(-2) - 3 = -4 - 3 = -7$	-7
0	$y = 2(0) - 3 = 0 - 3 = -3$	-3
2	$y = 2(2) - 3 = 4 - 3 = 1$	1
4	$y = 2(4) - 3 = 8 - 3 = 5$	5

x	y
-2	-7
0	-3
2	1
4	5

Represent the function with a verbal description.

Interpret the slope and y-intercept of the equation.

The output value is equal to three less than twice the input value.

Represent the function as a graph.

Graph the ordered pairs and draw a line through the points.

You could also draw a line with a slope of 2 and a y-intercept of -3.

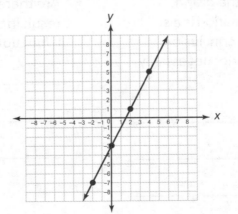

⫷ Connect

The following table and graph represent two different linear functions. Determine which has the greater rate of change.

x	y
−4	−3
−2	−2
0	−1
2	0
4	1

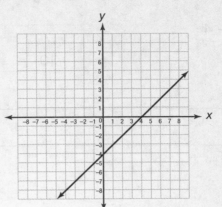

1

Determine the rate of change from the table.

Notice that as the x-values increase by 2, the y-values increase by 1.

$$\frac{\text{change in } y\text{-values}}{\text{change in } x\text{-values}} = \frac{1}{2}$$

The rate of change of the function represented by the table is $\frac{1}{2}$.

2

Determine the rate of change from the graph.

Use any two points on the graph.

Using (6, 2) for (x_2, y_2) and (0, −4) for (x_1, y_1):

$$\frac{2 - (-4)}{6 - 0} = \frac{6}{6} = 1$$

The rate of change of the function represented by the graph is 1.

3

Compare the rates of change.

$1 > \frac{1}{2}$

▶ The rate of change is greater for the function represented by the graph.

CHECK

Graph the function represented by the table of ordered pairs. You can graph the line on the same grid that shows the other function in order to visually confirm which rate of change is greater.

Practice

Determine which linear function has a greater rate of change. Then explain how you know.

1. $y = 3x - 4$

x	−7	−5	−3	−1	1	3
y	−10	−6	−2	2	6	10

_____

_____

> **REMEMBER** The *y*-intercept of a function is irrelevant when comparing the rates of change.

2. The output of a function is equal to the input divided by two.

x	−6	−3	0	3	6	9
y	−2	−1	0	1	2	3

_____

_____

3. $y = \frac{2}{3}x + 5$

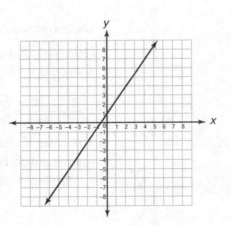

_____

_____

Determine which function has a greater y-intercept. Then explain how you know.

4.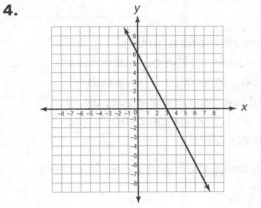

The output of a function is equal to four more than the product of the input and three.

_____

_____

_____

5. $y = \dfrac{3}{4}x + 2$

x	−2	−1	0	1	2	3
y	−10	−6	−2	2	6	10

_____

_____

Solve.

6. **COMPARE** Two functions are in the form $y = mx$. Explain what must be similar about the properties of the functions.

_____

_____

_____

7. **CONTRAST** One function has an equation in slope-intercept form: $y = x + 5$. Another function has an equation in standard form: $y + x = 5$. Explain what must be different about the properties of the functions. See if you can determine the differences without converting the equations to the same form.

_____

_____

_____

LESSON 15 Linear and Nonlinear Functions

UNDERSTAND The equation $y = mx + b$ represents a **linear function**. In this equation, x stands for the input values, y stands for the output values, m stands for the slope, and b stands for the y-intercept. The graph of a linear function is a nonvertical straight line. In a linear equation, no variable is raised to a power greater than 1. The graph of a **nonlinear function** will not produce a straight line.

The output value of a function is equal to four more than twice the input value. Represent the function in graph form, and then interpret the graph.

Translate the verbal description into an equation in slope-intercept form.

The output value of a function is equal to twice the input value plus four.

$$y \ = \ 2 \ \cdot \ x \ + \ 4$$

Choose values for x. Then substitute those values into the equation to find corresponding values for y.

$x = -4$	$x = -2$	$x = 0$	$x = 2$
$y = 2(\textbf{-4}) + 4$	$y = 2(\textbf{-2}) + 4$	$y = 2(\textbf{0}) + 4$	$y = 2(\textbf{2}) + 4$
$y = -8 + 4$	$y = -4 + 4$	$y = 0 + 4$	$y = 4 + 4$
$y = -4$	$y = 0$	$y = 4$	$y = 8$

Graph and interpret the function using the ordered pairs $(-4, -4)$, $(-2, 0)$, $(0, 4)$, and $(2, 8)$.

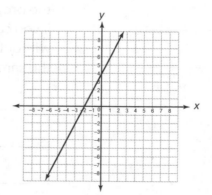

The graph of the function shows a straight line with a slope of 2 and a y-intercept of 4. The function is a linear function.

⊸ Connect

The following table represents a function.

x	−5	−3	−1	1	3	5
y	1	−1	−3	−5	−7	−9

Graph the function to determine if it is linear or nonlinear. Then use the graph to write the equation of the function.

1

Graph the function using the ordered pairs in the table.

Each pair of corresponding x- and y-values is an ordered pair for the function.

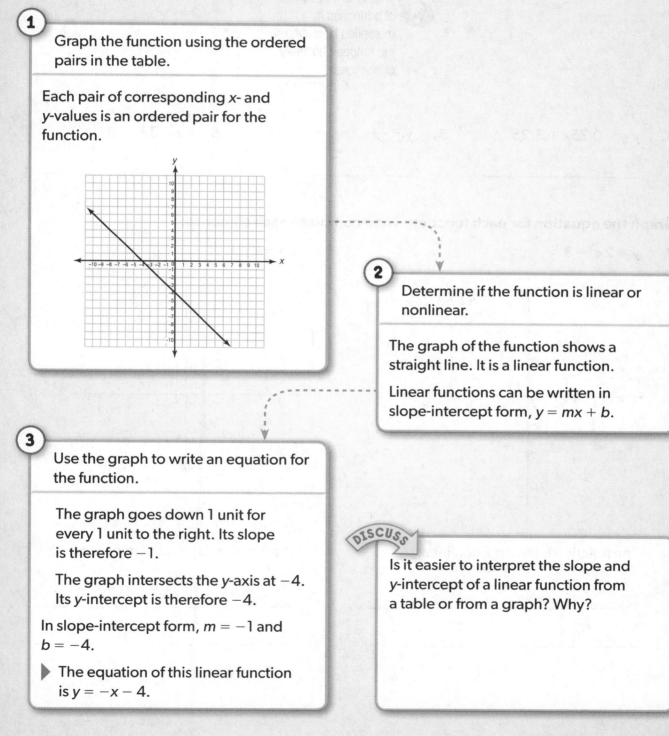

2

Determine if the function is linear or nonlinear.

The graph of the function shows a straight line. It is a linear function.

Linear functions can be written in slope-intercept form, $y = mx + b$.

3

Use the graph to write an equation for the function.

The graph goes down 1 unit for every 1 unit to the right. Its slope is therefore −1.

The graph intersects the y-axis at −4. Its y-intercept is therefore −4.

In slope-intercept form, $m = -1$ and $b = -4$.

▶ The equation of this linear function is $y = -x - 4$.

DISCUSS

Is it easier to interpret the slope and y-intercept of a linear function from a table or from a graph? Why?

Practice

Determine whether each equation represents a linear or nonlinear function.

1. $y = 5x - 8$

2. $y = x^2 + 2$

3. $y = \frac{1}{2}x$

_____

_____

_____

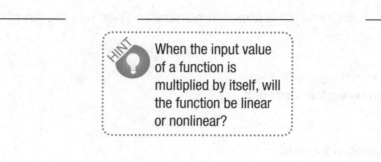

HINT When the input value of a function is multiplied by itself, will the function be linear or nonlinear?

4. $y = -0.75x + 3.25$

5. $y = \frac{10}{x}$

6. $y = 3x^2 - 3$

_____

_____

_____

Graph the equation for each function. Then complete each sentence.

7. $y = 2x^2 - 8$

8. $y = \frac{1}{3}x + 1$

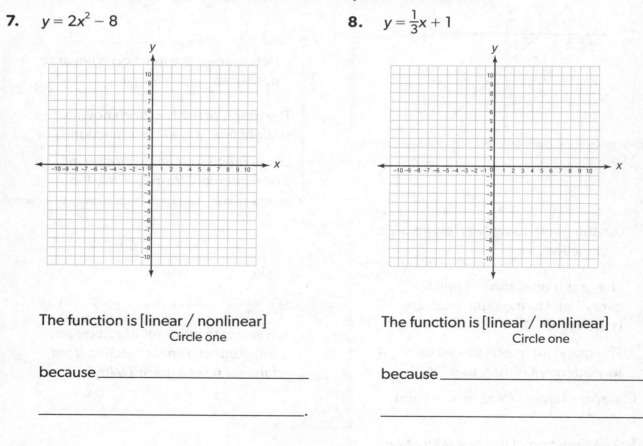

The function is [linear / nonlinear]
Circle one

because_____

_____.

The function is [linear / nonlinear]
Circle one

because_____

_____.

Choose the best answer.

9. Which equation represents a linear function?

    A. $y = -\frac{27}{53}x + \frac{1}{14}$

    B. $y = \frac{1}{2}x^2 + 2$

    C. $y = \sqrt{x}$

    D. $y = \frac{2}{x}$

10. Which of the following does **not** describe a linear function?

    A. the perimeter, p, of a square with side s: $p = 4s$

    B. the circumference, C, of a circle with radius r: $C = 2\pi r$

    C. the salary, s, of an employee making \$12.50 per hour, h: $s = 12.50h$

    D. the area, A, of a circle with radius r: $A = \pi r^2$

Solve.

11. EXPLAIN Does the equation $y = 4$ represent a linear function? Explain how you know.

_____

_____

_____

12. EXPLAIN Does the equation $x = 4$ represent a linear function? Explain how you know.

_____

_____

_____

13. DESCRIBE The speed of a skydiver falling to Earth, not considering air resistance, can be determined using the formula $a = 9.8s^2$, where a is the speed, in meters per second, and s is the number of seconds of free fall. Describe how you know whether or not the graph of a skydiver's speed over time would be a straight line.

_____

_____

_____

Using Functions to Model Relationships

You can use a linear function to model a real-life or mathematical relationship. To do this, determine the rate of change and the initial value (the starting point) of the situation. In a graph, the rate of change is the same as the slope and the initial value is the same as the *y*-intercept.

EXAMPLE A A water tank that holds 18 gallons leaks two gallons of water every minute. Determine the rate of change and initial value of the situation and use them to write an equation. Then graph the relationship.

1

Use the rate of change and initial value to write an equation in slope-intercept form.

Let *x* equal the number of minutes (the input value).

Let *y* equal the number of gallons of water in the tank (the output value).

The tank loses 2 gallons of water per minute. The rate of change is -2.
$m = -2$

There are 18 gallons of water in the tank at the beginning, so the initial value is 18. $b = 18$

Substitute the values of *m* and *b* into the equation $y = mx + b$.

$y = -2x + 18$

2

Graph the function.

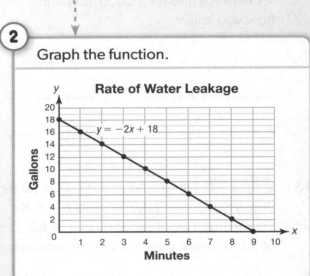

Rate of Water Leakage

$y = -2x + 18$

▶ The slope of the graph, -2, matches the rate of change. The *y*-intercept, 18, matches the initial value.

DISCUSS

What if the water were leaking at a rate of 3 gallons per minute? How would the graph change?

EXAMPLE B Determine the rate of change and initial value of the function in the table below. Use a graph to check your answer.

x	1	2	3	4	5
y	1	3	5	7	9

1

Determine the rate of change of the function.

As the x-values increase by 1, the y-values increase by 2.

$$\frac{\text{change in } y\text{-values}}{\text{change in } x\text{-values}} = \frac{2}{1}$$

The rate of change of the function represented by the table is 2.

2

Use the table and rate of change to find the initial value.

The equation of a function in slope-intercept form is $y = mx + b$.

Substitute the rate of change for m.
$y = 2x + b$

Substitute any ordered pair of x- and y-values from the table. For example, you can use (1, 1) or (4, 7).

Using (1, 1)   Using (4, 7)

$1 = 2(1) + b$ $7 = 2(4) + b$

$1 = 2 + b$ $7 = 8 + b$

$-1 = b$ $-1 = b$

The y-intercept (initial value) is −1.

▶ The equation of the function is $y = 2x - 1$. Its rate of change is 2 and its initial value is −1.

3

Check your answer.

Graph the equation $y = 2x - 1$ using the slope and y-intercept. Confirm that it passes through the points in the table.

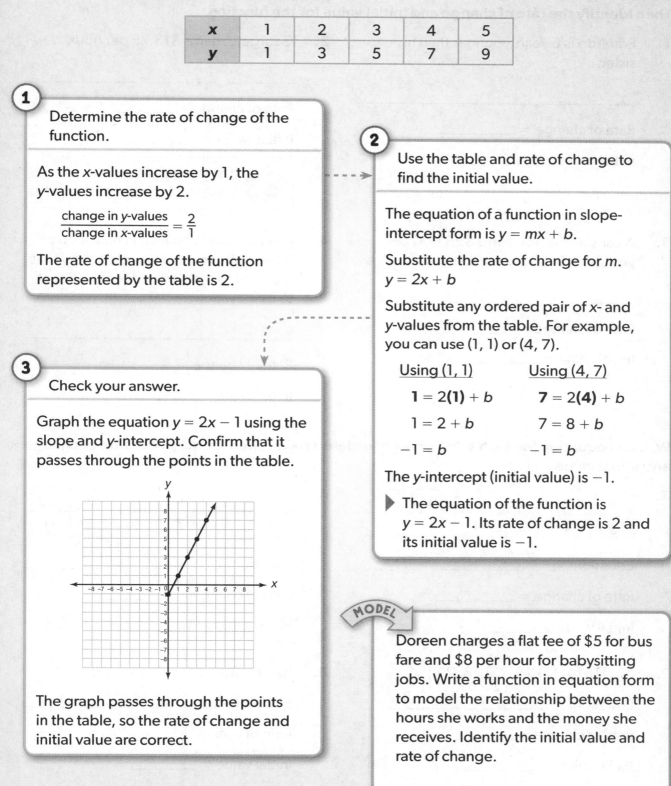

The graph passes through the points in the table, so the rate of change and initial value are correct.

MODEL

Doreen charges a flat fee of $5 for bus fare and $8 per hour for babysitting jobs. Write a function in equation form to model the relationship between the hours she works and the money she receives. Identify the initial value and rate of change.

Practice

Write an equation to represent each real-world situation, using *x* and *y* for the variables. Then identify the rate of change and initial value for the function.

1. Eduardo is 6 years younger than his sister.

_____

Rate of change = _____

Initial value = _____

2. Georgette earns $13.75 per hour.

_____

Rate of change = _____

Initial value = _____

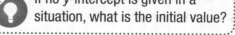
HINT If no *y*-intercept is given in a situation, what is the initial value?

3. A car salesperson earns $25,000 per year, plus $400 per car sold.

_____

Rate of change = _____

Initial value = _____

4. A skyscraper is built at an elevation of 24 feet above sea level. Each story that is added to the skyscraper adds 9 feet to its elevation.

_____

Rate of change = _____

Initial value = _____

Write an equation for each table or set of ordered pairs. Then identify each rate of change and initial value.

5.

x	2	4	6	8	10
y	2	3	4	5	6

Equation: _____

Rate of change = _____

Initial value = _____

6.

x	2	4	6	8	10
y	9	7	5	3	1

Equation: _____

Rate of change = _____

Initial value = _____

7. {(2, 11), (4, 17), (6, 23), (8, 29)}

Equation: _____

Rate of change = _____

Initial value = _____

8. {(2, 2), (3, 0), (4, −2), (5, −4)}

Equation: _____

Rate of change = _____

Initial value = _____

Write an equation for each graph. Then identify each rate of change and initial value.

9.

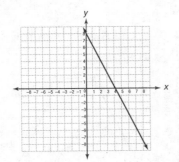

Equation: _____

Rate of change = _____

Initial value = _____

10.

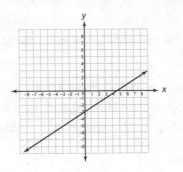

Equation: _____

Rate of change = _____

Initial value = _____

Choose the best answer.

11. What is the *y*-intercept for the function represented by the following table?

x	−2	0	2	4	6
y	3	4	5	6	7

A. −8

B. −2

C. 2

D. 4

12. Which function best represents the following relationship, where *x* is the number of gigabytes downloaded and *y* is the total monthly charge?

An internet provider charges $19.95 per month plus $7.50 for every gigabyte downloaded.

A. $y = 19.95x + 7.5$

B. $y = 7.5x + 19.95$

C. $y = x(7.5 + 19.95)$

D. $x = 7.5y + 19.95$

Solve.

13. EXPLAIN Explain how you can tell whether a linear function can be used to model a real-life relationship.

_____

_____

_____

14. RELATE Relate and compare the terms *slope, rate of change, y-intercept,* and *initial value.*

_____

_____

_____

17 Describing Functional Relationships from Graphs

A graph can provide additional information about a functional relationship.

EXAMPLE A Brett made a graph to show how far he traveled from home during a long-distance bike trip. Interpret the graph of this **piecewise function**.

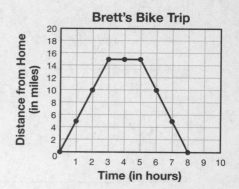

Brett's Bike Trip

1 Interpret the first segment of the function.

The function begins at the origin. That means that Brett has traveled 0 miles after 0 hours.

The first segment of the function is linear and increases as it moves from left to right.

The function passes through points (1, 5) and (2, 10). Its rate of change is $\frac{10-5}{2-1} = 5$.

Brett rode his bike 5 miles per hour away from his home during the first three hours.

2 Interpret the second segment of the function.

The second segment of the function is linear and stays constant from left to right. A horizontal line has a slope of 0. Brett neither increased nor decreased his distance from home during this time period, so he may have stopped riding his bike to take a break.

3 Interpret the third segment of the function.

The third segment of the function is linear and decreases as it moves from left to right.

The function passes through points (6, 10) and (8, 0). Its rate of change is $\frac{0-10}{8-6} = -\frac{10}{2} = -5$.

Brett rode his bike 5 miles per hour back toward his home during these three hours.

The function ends at (8, 0), where his distance from home is 0 miles. That means that Brett has returned home after 8 hours.

DISCUSS

What if the last segment of the graph went from (5, 15) to (10, 0)? How would the interpretation of the last part of the graph change?

EXAMPLE B The graph below represents the relationship between the side length of a square and the area of the square.

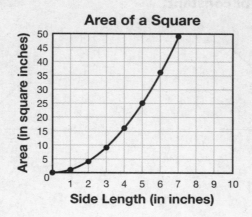

Area of a Square

Interpret the graph of this **quadratic function**.

1

Interpret the relationship of the function.

The relationship is nonlinear, and the graph increases as it moves from left to right. Because it is nonlinear, there is no constant rate of change and you cannot use two points to compute the slope.

2

Interpret how the output values change as the input values change.

Use a table.

Side Length	1	2	3	4	5	6	7
Area	1	4	9	16	25	36	49

As the side lengths (x-values) increase, the corresponding areas (y-values) increase, but at a greater rate. In the table above, as the x-values increase by 1, the corresponding y-values increase by 3, then by 5, then by 7, and so on.

▶ The graph shows that as the side length of a square increases, the area of the square also increases, but at a greater rate.

DISCUSS

Why is the graph representing the area of a square shown only in the first quadrant?

Practice

Identify each function as piecewise linear or nonlinear. Then identify where the functions are increasing, decreasing, or constant.

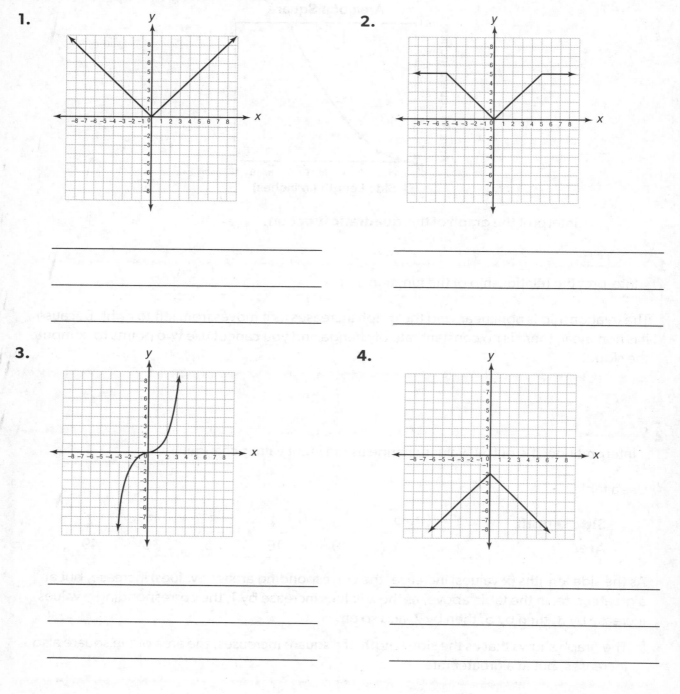

1.

2.

3.

4.

Sketch a graph based on this situation. Label the axes and justify your choices.

5. A scuba diver jumps into the water and descends at a constant rate for 4 minutes to a depth of 18 meters. She spends 24 minutes at that depth. She then ascends at a constant rate for 4 minutes to a depth of 6 meters, where she takes a 4-minute safety stop. She then ascends at a constant rate for an additional 4 minutes to reach the surface of the water.

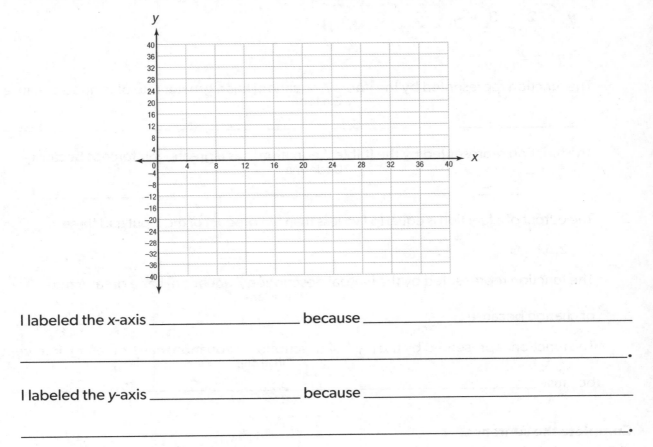

I labeled the x-axis _____ because _____

_____.

I labeled the y-axis _____ because _____

_____.

Solve.

6. **CREATE** Create a written scenario that would translate to a piecewise function.

    _____

    _____

    _____

7. **PREDICT** Without graphing the function, predict the shape of the graph representing the volume of a cube with side length s.

    _____

    _____

    _____

3 Review

Compare the properties of each function. Justify each answer.

1.

x	−10	−6	−2	2	6	10
y	2	3	4	5	6	7

$y = \frac{1}{2}x + 2$

The function represented by the [table / equation] has a greater rate of change because

Circle one

_____.

The function represented by the [table / equation] has a greater y-intercept because

Circle one

_____.

2. The output of a function is equal to five less than the product of the input and three.

$y = 2.5x − 3$

The function represented by the [verbal description / equation] has a greater rate

Circle one

of change because _____.

The function represented by the [verbal description / equation] has a greater y-intercept

Circle one

because _____.

Complete the sentence.

3. The relation $\{(−5, −8), (8, 5), (5, 3), (−5, 8)\}$ [does / does not] represent a function

Circle one

because _____.

Choose the best answer.

4. Which equation represents a linear function?

   A. $y = 8x^4$

   B. $y = −0.05x − 0.001$

   C. $y = 2x^2 + 5$

   D. $y = \sqrt[3]{x}$

5. Which set of ordered pairs does **not** represent a function?

   A. $\{(−6, 9), (−3, 3), (0, 3), (3, 9)\}$

   B. $\{(−2, 2), (−4, 2), (−6, 2), (−8, 2)\}$

   C. $\{(5, −1), (−1, 5), (5, 1), (1, −5)\}$

   D. $\{(10, −10), (5, −5), (−5, 5), (−10, 10)\}$

Use the following words to describe the graph of each function: *linear, nonlinear, piecewise, increasing, decreasing, constant.*

6.

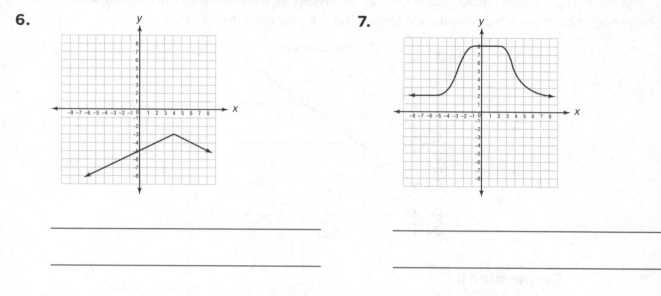

7.

_____

_____

_____

_____

_____

_____

Write an equation to represent each real-world situation, using x and y for the unknown variables. Then identify the rate of change and initial value of each function.

8. A credit card company charges vendors a $0.35 fee for any purchase, plus 2.5% of the purchase.

_____

Rate of change = _____

Initial value = _____

9. Tina earns $25.95 per hour, plus a consulting fee of $50.

_____

Rate of change = _____

Initial value = _____

Choose the best answer.

10. Which set of ordered pairs represents a linear function?

A. {(−6, −2), (−3, −1), (0, 1), (1, 3)}

B. {(−8, 0), (−8, −3), (−8, −6), (−8, −9)}

C. {(−1, 1), (0, 2), (1, 4), (2, 7)}

D. {(−4, −1), (−1, 1), (2, 3), (8, 7)}

11. What is the initial value of the function represented by the following table?

x	2	3	4	5	6
y	2	0	−2	−4	−6

A. −6

B. −2

C. 3

D. 6

Use the situation, graph, and table below to answer questions 12–14.

The predicted profits of two corporations are modeled by the following representations. The *y*-intercept of each representation shows the data for the current year.

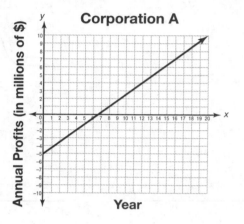

Corporation A

Annual Profits (in millions of $)

Year

Corporation B

Year, *x*	0	2	4	6	8	10	12	14	16	18	20
Annual Profits (in $millions), *y*	−5	−1	−3	−1	3	5	3	7	9	7	10

12. Determine whether each corporation's predicted model represents a function. Explain your answers.

_____

_____

13. Determine whether each corporation's predicted model represents a linear or nonlinear function. Explain your answers.

_____

_____

14. For a model above that represents a linear function, determine the initial value and rate of change. Then describe the rate of change and initial value in terms of the context of the problem.

_____

_____

_____

_____

_____

Describing Functions

Work in groups of three. Each person needs three 4-quadrant coordinate planes.

One student in the group should write a sentence to describe a function using words. Another student in the group should write a function in the form $y = mx + b$, where m, x, and b are all nonzero values. The third student in the group should sketch a function on a coordinate grid. The representations can represent a variety of functions, including increasing, decreasing, linear, nonlinear, and piecewise. When you are done, make two copies of your representation. Give the copies to the other students in your group. Then answer the following questions.

1 How do you know that the other students' models represent functions?

_____

_____

2 For the function that was described verbally, use a coordinate plane to sketch the function.

3 For the function that was described with an equation, use a coordinate plane to sketch the function. Explain how you were able to tell the shape of the function before graphing it.

_____

_____

4 Describe each function with as much detail as possible. Identify the rate of change and y-intercept. Determine whether the function is linear or nonlinear, increasing or decreasing, quadratic, piecewise, and so on.

_____

_____

_____

Once the questions have been answered, compare the properties of the functions. Determine which function has the greatest rate of change and which function has the greatest y-intercept.

_____

_____

Grade 7 RP

Analyze proportional relationships and use them to solve real-world and mathematical problems.

Grade 7 EE

Solve real-life and mathematical problems using numerical and algebraic expressions and equations.

Grade 7 G

Draw, construct and describe geometrical figures and describe the relationships between them.

Solve real-life and mathematical problems involving angle measure, area, surface area, and volume.

Grade 8 G

Understand congruence and similarity using physical models, transparencies, or geometry software.

Understand and apply the Pythagorean Theorem.

Solve real-world and mathematical problems involving volume of cylinders, cones and spheres.

Domain 4
Geometry

LESSON 18

Properties of Rotations, Reflections, and Translations

UNDERSTAND A **rigid motion** changes the position of a figure without changing its shape or size. A sequence of rigid motions can transform a figure into a **congruent** figure. Each point on the original figure matches a corresponding point on the transformed figure, called the **image**. If the vertices of the original figure are labeled with letters, such as *ABCD*, then the vertices of the image will be labeled with a prime symbol, ('), as in *A'B'C'D'*.

A **rotation** is a turn of a figure about a point.
Triangle *J'K'L'* is a 90°-clockwise rotation of triangle *JKL* about point *J*.

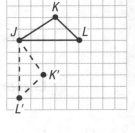

A **reflection** is a flip of a figure over a point or line.
Quadrilateral *M'N'O'P'* is a reflection of quadrilateral *MNOP* over the vertical line.

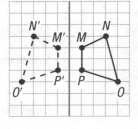

A **translation** is a slide of a figure to a new location.
Pentagon *A'B'C'D'E'* is a translation of pentagon *ABCDE* 4 units down and 5 units to the left.

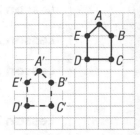

You can demonstrate the congruence of two figures by using a rigid motion or a sequence of rigid motions to make the figures coincide.

⊏ Connect

Describe the rigid motion that will make the two intersecting lines coincide.

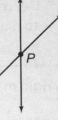

1 | Trace the vertical line on tracing paper.

2 | Rotate it around point *P* so that it completely covers the slanted line.

A clockwise rotation of 45° is needed. You can use a protractor to verify the degree of rotation.

▶ A 45°-clockwise rotation around point *P* can be used to make the two lines coincide.

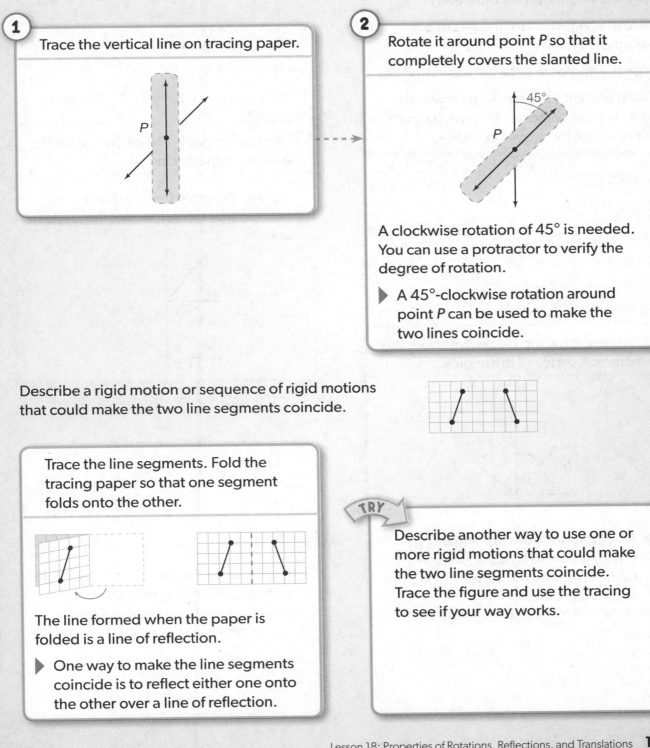

Describe a rigid motion or sequence of rigid motions that could make the two line segments coincide.

Trace the line segments. Fold the tracing paper so that one segment folds onto the other.

The line formed when the paper is folded is a line of reflection.

▶ One way to make the line segments coincide is to reflect either one onto the other over a line of reflection.

TRY Describe another way to use one or more rigid motions that could make the two line segments coincide. Trace the figure and use the tracing to see if your way works.

EXAMPLE A Describe a sequence of rigid motions that could be used to make the 60° angles coincide.

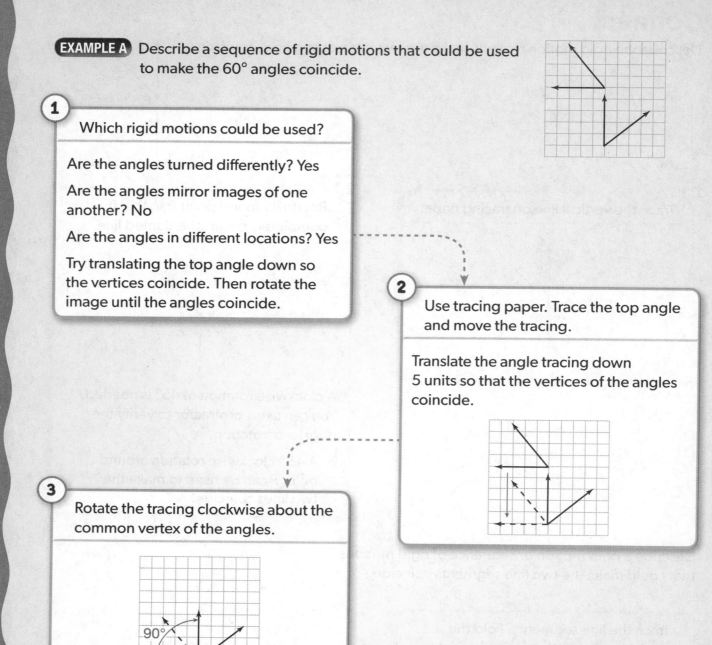

1

Which rigid motions could be used?

Are the angles turned differently? Yes

Are the angles mirror images of one another? No

Are the angles in different locations? Yes

Try translating the top angle down so the vertices coincide. Then rotate the image until the angles coincide.

2

Use tracing paper. Trace the top angle and move the tracing.

Translate the angle tracing down 5 units so that the vertices of the angles coincide.

3

Rotate the tracing clockwise about the common vertex of the angles.

▶ A translation of the top angle 5 units down, followed by a 90°-clockwise rotation around the vertex, makes the angles coincide.

DISCUSS

If you reverse the order of the two rigid motions (first rotate, then translate), would the angles coincide? Explain why or why not.

EXAMPLE B Describe how a reflection and a translation could be used to make parallel lines *AB* and *CD* coincide with parallel lines *A″B″* and *C″D″*.

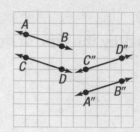

1

Reflect $\overleftrightarrow{AB}$ and $\overleftrightarrow{CD}$ over a line to create a mirror image of the two lines.

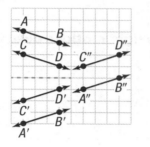

Lines *AB* and *CD* can be reflected over a horizontal line to form lines *A′B′* and *C′D′*. Point *A* corresponds to point *A′*, point *B* corresponds to point *B′*, point *C* corresponds to point *C′*, and point *D* corresponds to point *D′*.

2

Look at the diagram below.

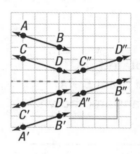

Visualize sliding line *A′B′* and line *C′D′* so that each point moves 5 units to the right and 3 units up to make parallel lines *A′B′* and *C′D′* coincide with parallel lines *A″B″* and *C″D″*.

▶ A reflection across a horizontal line below line *CD*, followed by a translation to the right and up, makes parallel lines *AB* and *CD* coincide with parallel lines *A″B″* and *C″D″*.

TRY

Describe how a reflection and a translation could be used to make parallel lines *AB* and *CD* coincide with parallel lines *A″B″* and *C″D″*. Use *Math Tool: Grid Paper* to sketch the steps.

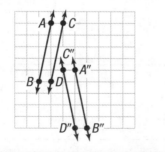

Practice

Identify the type of rigid motion needed to make the two figures coincide in one step.

1.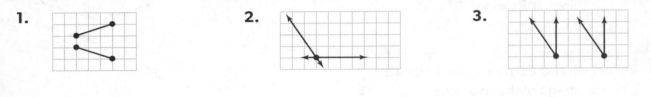

2.

3.

_____   _____   _____

Identify the line segment that could coincide with $\overline{AB}$ if the rigid motions described are performed.

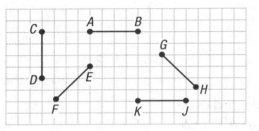

4. $\overline{AB}$ is rotated 180°
    around point B and
    then translated down.

    _____

5. $\overline{AB}$ is rotated 90°
    clockwise around
    point A and then
    reflected across a
    vertical line.

    _____

6. $\overline{AB}$ is rotated 135°
    clockwise around
    point A and then
    translated down.

    _____

> **REMEMBER** You can use
> tracing paper and a protractor
> to help visualize the rigid
> motions described.

Write true or false for each statement. If false, rewrite the statement so it is true.

7. Rigid motions do not change the shape of a figure.

_____

8. Rigid motions may change the size of a figure.

_____

Describe in detail how one or more rigid motions could be used to make the leftmost figure coincide with the rightmost figure. Use the fewest rigid motions possible.

9.

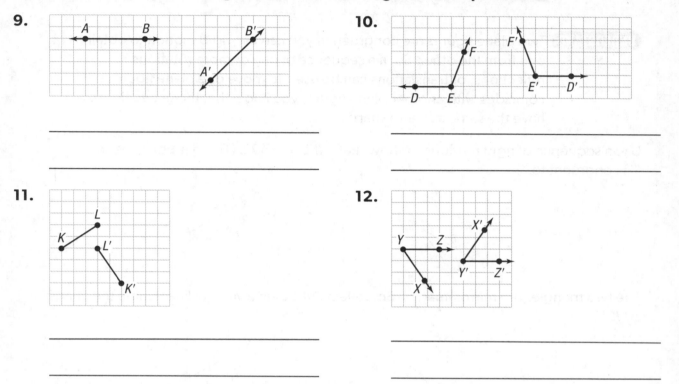

_____

_____

10.

_____

_____

11.

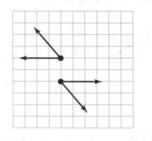

_____

_____

12.

_____

_____

Solve.

13. **DESCRIBE** Use words and/or drawings to describe two different sequences of rigid motions that could be used to make the 50° angles shown coincide.

_____

_____

_____

14. **WRITE MATH** Reflect the pair of parallel lines over the dashed line. Then explain how a rotation and a reflection can be used to move those reflected images so that they coincide with the original parallel lines.

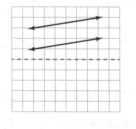

_____

_____

_____

Understanding Congruence of Two-Dimensional Figures (Using Rigid Motions)

UNDERSTAND Two plane figures are congruent if you can use rigid motion to obtain one from the other. So, if a sequence of one or more rotations, reflections, or translations can be used to move one plane figure so it coincides with another plane figure, you know that those two figures have the same size and shape.

Use a sequence of rigid motions to show that △*JKL* ≅ △*PQR*. (The symbol ≅ means "is congruent to.")

The two triangles are mirror images. So, reflect △*JKL* over a vertical line. Name the image △*J'K'L'*.

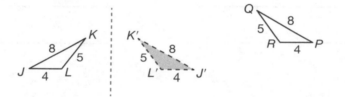

The reflected image of each segment is equal in length to the original segment. For example, $\overline{JL}$ is 4 units long and so is its image, *J'L'*.

The reflected image of △*JKL* and △*PQR* are in different locations. So, translate the reflected image up and to the right so it completely covers △*PQR*. Name it △*J"K"L"*.

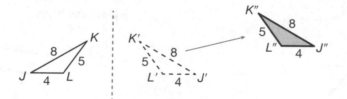

Triangle *J"K"L"* shows that rigid motions moved $\overline{JK}$ onto $\overline{PQ}$, $\overline{KL}$ onto $\overline{QR}$, and $\overline{JL}$ onto $\overline{PR}$.

They also moved ∠*J* onto ∠*P*, ∠*K* onto ∠*Q*, and ∠*L* onto ∠*R*.

Corresponding line segments are congruent, and corresponding angles are congruent.

A reflection over a vertical line, followed by a translation up and to the right, makes △*JKL* coincide with △*PQR*. △*JKL* ≅ △*PQR*

← Connect

Describe two different ways to show that quadrilateral *ABCD* is congruent to quadrilateral *WXYZ*.

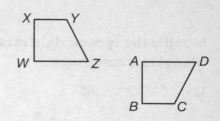

1 Reflect quadrilateral *ABCD* over a horizontal line.

2 Slide the reflected image to the left so that it completely covers quadrilateral *WXYZ*.

▶ One way of showing that *ABCD* ≅ *WXYZ* is to reflect quadrilateral *ABCD* over $\overline{AD}$, and then translate that image to the left.

3 Rotate quadrilateral *ABCD* 180° counterclockwise around point *A*.

180°

4 Reflect the rotated image across a vertical line so that it completely covers quadrilateral *WXYZ*.

▶ Another way of showing that *ABCD* ≅ *WXYZ* is to rotate quadrilateral *ABCD* 180° counterclockwise around point *A*, and then reflect the image over a vertical line.

DISCUSS

Is it possible to use rigid motions to obtain quadrilateral *WXYZ* from quadrilateral *ABCD* without using at least one reflection? Explain why or why not.

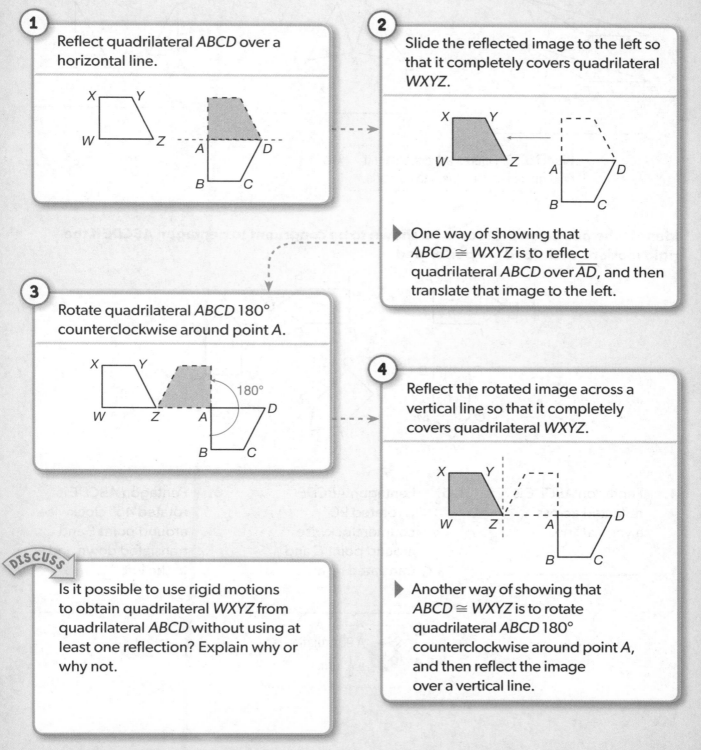

Practice

Identify the type of rigid motion that could be used to show in one step that each pair of triangles is congruent.

1. △NPQ ≅ △RST

2. △HJK ≅ △LMK

3. △ABC ≅ △DFG

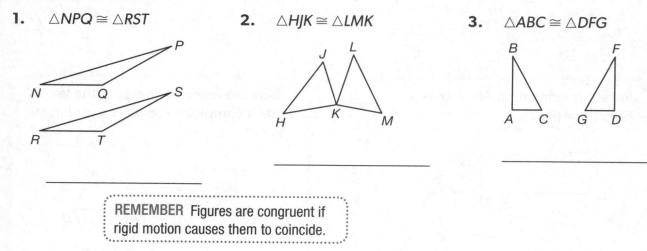

_____

_____

_____

> **REMEMBER** Figures are congruent if rigid motion causes them to coincide.

Identify the pentagon that could be shown to be congruent to pentagon ABCDE if the rigid motions described are performed.

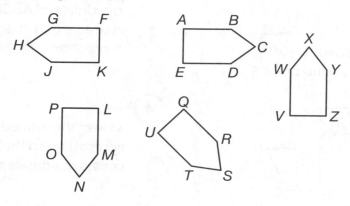

4. Pentagon *ABCDE* is reflected across a vertical line.

_____

5. Pentagon *ABCDE* is rotated 90° counterclockwise around point *C* and translated right.

_____

6. Pentagon *ABCDE* is rotated 45° clockwise around point *E* and translated down and to the left.

_____

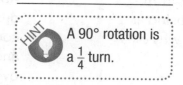

> **HINT** A 90° rotation is a $\frac{1}{4}$ turn.

Fill in each blank with an appropriate word or words.

7. Two figures are congruent if one figure can be obtained from the other using a sequence of translations, _____, or _____.

8. Rigid motions can be used to move the sides of a figure onto congruent, corresponding _____ of a congruent figure.

9. Rigid motions can be used to move angles in a figure onto congruent, corresponding _____ in a congruent figure.

Describe in detail how a sequence of rigid motions could be used to show that each pair of figures is congruent.

10.

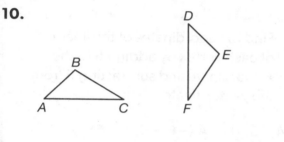

_____

11.

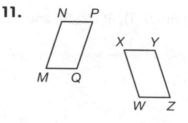

_____

Solve.

12. **DESCRIBE** Use words and/or drawings to describe two different sequences of rigid motions that could be used to show that the two isosceles trapezoids are congruent.

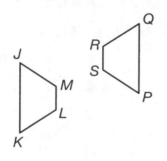

_____

_____

13. **PROVE** Right triangle *ABC* and acute triangle *XYZ* are not congruent.

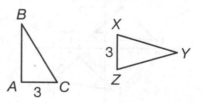

Use words and/or drawings to describe a sequence of rigid motions that will prove they are not congruent.

_____

_____

Rigid Motion on the Coordinate Plane

EXAMPLE A The rule below means add 5 to the *x*-coordinate and subtract 6 from the *y*-coordinate of an ordered pair.

$$(x, y) \rightarrow (x + 5, y - 6)$$

Use the rule to translate $\triangle ABC$. Describe the translation.

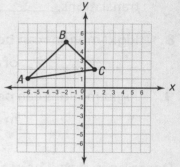

1

Identify the coordinates of the vertices of $\triangle ABC$.

The vertices are: $A(-6, 1)$, $B(-2, 5)$, and $C(1, 2)$.

2

Find the coordinates of the image of each vertex by adding 5 to the *x*-coordinate and subtracting 6 from the *y*-coordinate.

$A(-6, 1) \rightarrow A'(-6 + \mathbf{5}, 1 - \mathbf{6}) \rightarrow$
$A'(\mathbf{-1}, \mathbf{-5})$

$B(-2, 5) \rightarrow B'(-2 + \mathbf{5}, 5 - \mathbf{6}) \rightarrow$
$B'(\mathbf{3}, \mathbf{-1})$

$C(1, 2) \rightarrow C'(1 + \mathbf{5}, 2 - \mathbf{6}) \rightarrow C'(\mathbf{6}, \mathbf{-4})$

3

Plot and connect those vertices to form $\triangle A'B'C'$.

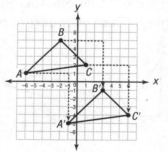

▶ The graph shows the translated image $\triangle A'B'C'$, which is the result of a translation of $\triangle ABC$ 5 units to the right and 6 units down.

TRY

Now use the following rule to translate $\triangle ABC$ to form $\triangle A''B''C''$:

$$(x, y) \rightarrow (x - 5, y + 6)$$

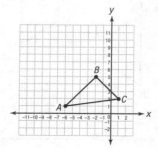

Explain how the translation differs from the one in the example.

EXAMPLE B Reflect △DEF across the x-axis. Then make a generalization about figures that are reflected across the x-axis.

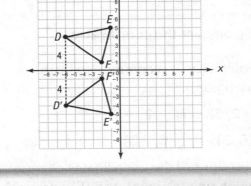

1

Identify the coordinates of the vertices of △DEF.

The vertices are: $D(-6, 4)$, $E(-1, 5)$, and $F(-2, 1)$.

2

Reflect each vertex across the x-axis and connect them to form △D′E′F′.

Vertex D is on the line $x = -6$ and is 4 units above the x-axis. Its image, point D′, is also on the line $x = -6$, but it is 4 units below the x-axis.

Vertex E and its image, vertex E′, are each 5 units from the x-axis.

Vertex F and its image, vertex F′, are each 1 unit from the x-axis.

3

Compare the coordinates.

$D(-6, 4) \rightarrow D'(-6, -\mathbf{4})$

$E(-1, 5) \rightarrow E'(-1, -\mathbf{5})$

$F(-2, 1) \rightarrow F'(-2, -\mathbf{1})$

After the reflection, the x-coordinate stays the same, but the sign of the y-coordinate changes.

▶ The reflected image, △D′E′F′, is shown above. The reflection of a point (x, y) across the x-axis results in the point $(x, -y)$.

TRY

On the coordinate plane below, reflect △DEF across the y-axis. Then make a generalization about figures that are reflected across the y-axis.

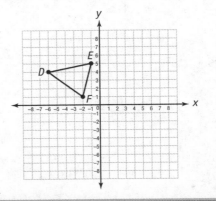

EXAMPLE C Rotate △GHJ 180° around the origin. Then make a generalization about rotating a figure around the origin.

1

Identify the coordinates of the vertices of △GHJ.

The vertices are: G(0, 0), H(2, 5), and J(6, 3).

2

Rotate each vertex of △GHJ 180° clockwise around the origin. Then connect the vertices to form △GH'J'.

Since point G is at the origin, this is the same as a $\frac{1}{2}$ turn around point G.

3

Compare the coordinates.

Point G(0, 0) is common to both triangles.

$H(2, 5) \rightarrow H'(-2, -5)$

$J(6, 3) \rightarrow J'(-6, -3)$

The signs of the coordinates change when points are rotated 180° around the origin.

▶ The rotated image, △GH'J', is shown above. The rotation of a point (x, y) 180° around the origin results in the point (−x, −y).

DISCUSS

Look at the triangles below. Compare the coordinates of the vertices of △GHJ with the coordinates of the vertices of △GH"J". Then use the two sets of coordinates to make a generalization about the result of a 90°-counterclockwise rotation around the origin.

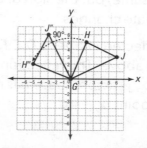

⚙ Problem Solving

READ

Mr. Miller wants to move an L-shaped bookcase in his classroom from its current location to a new location. The diagram shows a map of his classroom. Describe a sequence of rigid motions that could be used to relocate the bookcase.

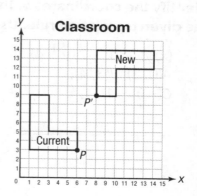

PLAN

The two bookcases are turned differently, so you will need to use a _____.

They are in different _____, so you will need to use a translation as well.

Use a _____ followed by a translation.

SOLVE

First, _____ the bookcase labeled "current" _____ degrees clockwise around point P. Draw that image on the grid.

Consider how point P must be translated to form the image, point P'.

If point P is translated 2 units to the _____ and _____ units up, it will move onto point P'. So, the translation rule is $(x, y) \rightarrow (x + \boxed{}, y \boxed{} 6)$.

CHECK

A _____ degree rotation is a $\frac{1}{4}$ turn, and a $\frac{1}{4}$ turn could move the bookcase labeled "current" so it is turned in the same way as the bookcase labeled "new."

The bookcase labeled "new" is higher and farther to the _____ on the grid, so a translation up and to the _____ is also reasonable.

▶ A _____ of the current bookcase _____ degrees clockwise around point P, followed by a translation of 2 units to the _____ and _____ units up, could be used.

Practice

Identify the coordinates of the images of the given points, using the prime (') symbol and the given translation rule. Use *Math Tool: Coordinate Plane*.

1. $(x, y) \rightarrow (x + 2, y + 4)$
$A(0, 3), B(3, 4),$
$C(-6, -4)$

_____

2. $(x, y) \rightarrow (x + 1, y - 5)$
$D(4, 5), E(-1, 4),$
$F(-9, -10)$

_____

3. $(x, y) \rightarrow (x - 7, y - 3)$
$G(8, 9), H(6, -4),$
$J(-5, 5)$

_____

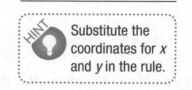

HINT

Substitute the coordinates for x and y in the rule.

Use the prime (') symbol to identify each image and give the coordinates of the image. Use *Math Tool: Coordinate Plane*.

4. $K(2, 3), L(0, -5),$
$M(-3, -7)$ reflected
over the x-axis

_____

5. $N(6, 5), P(-3, 4),$
$Q(-1, -9)$ reflected
over the y-axis

_____

6. $R(4, 5), S(-2, 5),$
$T(7, -8)$ rotated 180°
around the origin

_____

> **REMEMBER** The reflection of (x, y) across the y-axis is $(-x, y)$.

Use the grid on the right to perform each described rigid motion.

7. Reflect $\triangle XYZ$ across the x-axis to form $\triangle X'Y'Z'$.

8. Translate $\triangle XYZ$ using the following rule to form $\triangle X''Y''Z''$: $(x, y) \rightarrow (x - 8, y + 9)$.

9. Rotate $\triangle XYZ$ 90° clockwise around point X to form $\triangle XY'''Z'''$.

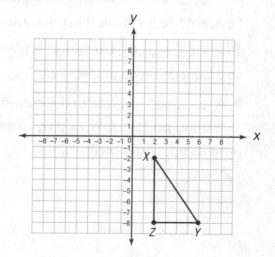

Graph the result of each described sequence of rigid motions, showing each step. Use prime (') symbols to name each image.

10. Triangle *BCD* is rotated 180° around point *B* and then translated using this rule: $(x, y) \rightarrow (x - 1, y - 5)$.

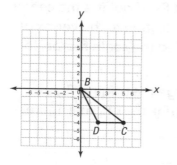

11. Trapezoid *FGHJ* is rotated 90° clockwise around point *J* and then reflected across the *x*-axis.

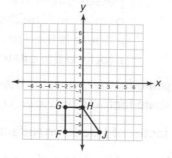

Solve.

12. DRAW Can you rotate △*WXY* 180° clockwise around the origin even though the origin is not a point on the triangle? If so, draw the image △*W′X′Y′* and compare its coordinates to those of the original figure. If not, use a drawing to show why not.

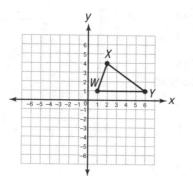

_____

_____

13. DESCRIBE An artist used drawing software to draw Design 1 on her computer. She wants to use a sequence of rigid motions to transform that design so it looks like and is in the same location as Design 2.

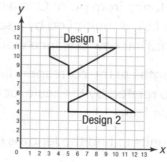

Use words and/or drawings to describe a sequence she could use.

_____

_____

Dilations on the Coordinate Plane

UNDERSTAND A **dilation** is a nonrigid transformation that changes the size, but not the shape, of a figure. Imagine a ray that starts at a fixed point and passes through each point on a figure. That fixed point is the center of dilation. The distance from the center of dilation to the vertex of a figure is then multiplied by a number, called the **scale factor**, to produce the dilated image.

• If the scale factor is greater than 1, the dilation will enlarge the original figure.
• If the scale factor is between 0 and 1, the dilation will shrink the original figure.

A scale factor of 1 does not affect the size of a figure.

Rectangle *ABCD* was dilated to form rectangle *A'B'C'D'*. The center of dilation was at the origin. What scale factor was used?

Visualize the dilation. Draw dashed rays to help you.

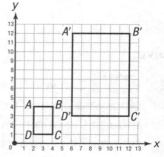

Each ray starts at the origin, *O*, and passes through a vertex of rectangle *ABCD*.

It also passes through the corresponding vertex on rectangle *A'B'C'D'*.

The distance from point *O* to a point on rectangle *ABCD*, such as *OA*, is multiplied by a scale factor to produce the dilation. That new distance would be the distance *OA'*.

The lengths of the corresponding sides of the rectangles are also related by the scale factor. Use those lengths to find the scale factor.

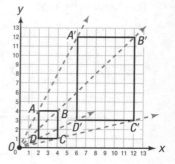

Count units to find the lengths of two horizontal sides.

For example, $AB = 2$ units and $A'B' = 6$ units.
Since $2 \times 3 = 6$, $\overline{A'B'}$ is 3 times as long as $\overline{AB}$.

Count units to find the lengths of two vertical sides.

For example, $AD = 3$ units and $A'D' = 9$ units.
Since $3 \times 3 = 9$, $\overline{A'D'}$ is 3 times as long as $\overline{AD}$.

The scale factor is 3.

←€ Connect

Draw the image of △*HJK* after a dilation by a scale factor of $\frac{1}{2}$. Use the origin as the center of dilation.

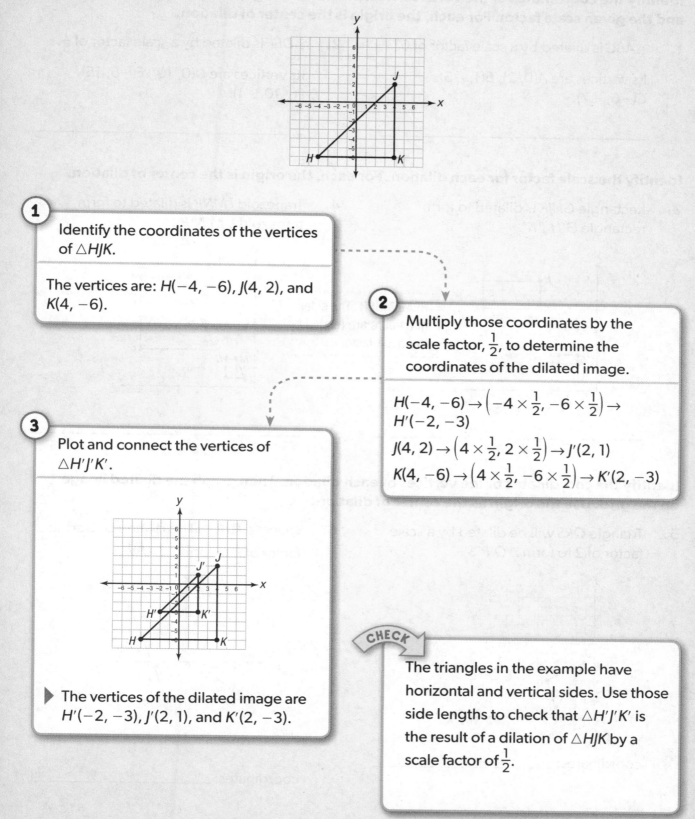

1

Identify the coordinates of the vertices of △*HJK*.

The vertices are: *H*(−4, −6), *J*(4, 2), and *K*(4, −6).

2

Multiply those coordinates by the scale factor, $\frac{1}{2}$, to determine the coordinates of the dilated image.

$H(-4, -6) \rightarrow \left(-4 \times \frac{1}{2}, -6 \times \frac{1}{2}\right) \rightarrow H'(-2, -3)$

$J(4, 2) \rightarrow \left(4 \times \frac{1}{2}, 2 \times \frac{1}{2}\right) \rightarrow J'(2, 1)$

$K(4, -6) \rightarrow \left(4 \times \frac{1}{2}, -6 \times \frac{1}{2}\right) \rightarrow K'(2, -3)$

3

Plot and connect the vertices of △*H′J′K′*.

▶ The vertices of the dilated image are *H′*(−2, −3), *J′*(2, 1), and *K′*(2, −3).

CHECK

The triangles in the example have horizontal and vertical sides. Use those side lengths to check that △*H′J′K′* is the result of a dilation of △*HJK* by a scale factor of $\frac{1}{2}$.

Practice

Identify the coordinates of the vertices of each dilated image, using the prime (') symbol and the given scale factor. For each, the origin is the center of dilation.

1. △ABC is dilated by a scale factor of 6.

Its vertices are A(0, 2), B(1, −5), C(−6, −7).

_____

2. △DEF is dilated by a scale factor of $\frac{1}{5}$.

Its vertices are D(0, 10), E(−5, 15), F(−10, −1).

_____

Identify the scale factor for each dilation. For each, the origin is the center of dilation.

3. Rectangle GHJK is dilated to form rectangle G′H′J′K′.

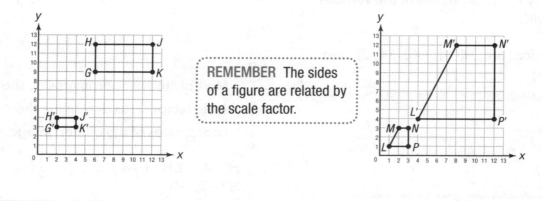

REMEMBER The sides of a figure are related by the scale factor.

4. Trapezoid LMNP is dilated to form trapezoid L′M′N′P′.

_____

Identify the coordinates of the vertices of each dilation. Then graph the dilated image on the grid. Use the origin as the center of dilation.

5. Triangle QRS will be dilated by a scale factor of 2 to form △Q′R′S′.

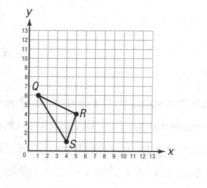

coordinates: _____

6. Triangle TUV will be dilated by a scale factor of $\frac{1}{2}$ to form △T′U′V′.

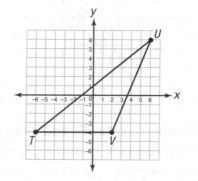

coordinates: _____

Graph the result of each sequence of a dilation followed by a rigid motion, showing each step. Use prime (') symbols to name each image. Use the origin as the center of dilation.

7. Parallelogram *WXYZ* will be dilated by a scale factor of $\frac{1}{4}$ and then translated 8 units up.

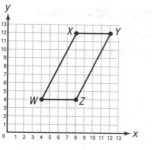

8. Triangle *CDE* will be dilated by a scale factor of 3 and then reflected over the *x*-axis.

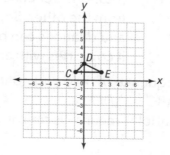

Solve. Use the origin as the center of dilation.

9. **COMPARE** The scale drawing shows a rectangular children's pool at a community center.

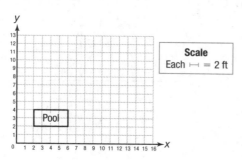

An architect uses the origin as the center of dilation and dilates this figure by a scale factor of 2.5. The architect's new drawing shows the scale and location of a larger pool that will be built at the same site. Draw the larger pool. Then compare the perimeters of the two pools. Show or explain your work.

_____

_____

_____

10. **DESCRIBE** Max drew a quadrilateral as a logo for the school newsletter. He decided to dilate it by a scale factor of $\frac{2}{3}$ to make it smaller, and then drew the second figure shown.

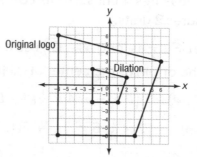

Describe the error he made during his dilation. Then draw the logo as it would look if dilated correctly. Show your work.

_____

_____

_____

Understanding Similarity of Two-Dimensional Figures (Using Transformations)

UNDERSTAND **Similar** figures have the same shape, but not necessarily the same size. Two plane figures are similar if you can use a sequence of rotations, reflections, translations, and dilations to obtain one from the other. So, if a sequence of one or more rigid motions and dilations can be used to transform one plane figure so that it coincides with another plane figure, the figures are similar.

Use a sequence of rigid and nonrigid motions to show that $\triangle ABC \sim \triangle DEF$.
(The symbol $\sim$ means "is similar to.")

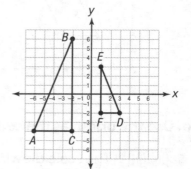

Which rigid and nonrigid motions are needed?

The two triangles are different sizes, so a dilation will be needed. Once dilated, the triangles will look like mirror images, so a reflection will also be needed.

Reflect $\triangle ABC$ across the y-axis. Name the image $\triangle A'B'C'$.

The figures are still different sizes, so dilate $\triangle A'B'C'$.

$\overline{A'C'}$ measures 4 units and its corresponding side $\overline{DF}$ measures 2 units.

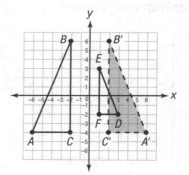

Since $\overline{DF}$ is $\frac{1}{2}$ as long as $\overline{A'C'}$, use a scale factor of $\frac{1}{2}$. Use the origin as the center of dilation.

$A'(6, -4) \to \left(6 \times \frac{1}{2}, -4 \times \frac{1}{2}\right) \to D(3, -2)$

$B'(2, 6) \to \left(2 \times \frac{1}{2}, 6 \times \frac{1}{2}\right) \to E(1, 3)$

$C'(2, -4) \to \left(2 \times \frac{1}{2}, -4 \times \frac{1}{2}\right) \to F(1, -2)$

A reflection of $\triangle ABC$ across the y-axis, followed by a dilation by a scale factor of $\frac{1}{2}$ with the origin as the center of dilation, shows that $\triangle ABC \sim \triangle DEF$.

To show that $\triangle ABC \sim \triangle DEF$, you could also start with $\triangle DEF$ and reflect it over the y-axis to create the image $\triangle D'E'F'$. In this case, you would use a scale factor of 2 to make the image $\triangle D'E'F'$ coincide with $\triangle ABC$.

⊣€ Connect

Is rectangle *GHJK* similar to rectangle *PQRS*? Use rigid and nonrigid motions to justify your answer.

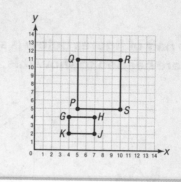

1

Compare the sides of the rectangles.

In rectangle *GHJK*, the shorter sides are vertical.

In rectangle *PQRS*, the shorter sides are horizontal.

Use a rotation to try to orient the rectangles the same way.

2

Rotate rectangle *GHJK* 90° counterclockwise around point *K*.

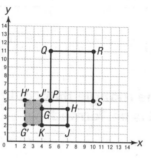

The two rectangles do not look similar. Let's use a dilation to confirm that they are not similar.

3

Find a scale factor that relates a pair of corresponding sides of the rectangles. Use that scale factor to dilate rectangle *G'H'J'K*.

$\overline{G'K}$ = 2 units and $\overline{PS}$ = 5 units.

$5 \div 2 = 2.5$, so use a scale factor of 2.5. Use the origin as the center of dilation.

$G'(2, 2) \rightarrow (2 \times 2.5, 2 \times 2.5) \rightarrow (5, 5)$

Those are the coordinates of point *P*. Find the other coordinates of the dilation.

$H'(2, 5) \rightarrow (2 \times 2.5, 5 \times 2.5) \rightarrow (5, 12.5)$

$J'(4, 5) \rightarrow (4 \times 2.5, 5 \times 2.5) \rightarrow (10, 12.5)$

$K(4, 2) \rightarrow (4 \times 2.5, 2 \times 2.5) \rightarrow (10, 5)$

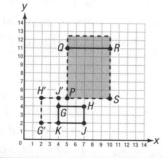

4

Compare the rectangles.

The dilated image has the same width as rectangle *PQRS*, but its length is 1.5 units greater. The rectangles have different shapes.

▶ A rotation and a dilation show that rectangles *GHJK* and *PQRS* are different shapes. They are not similar.

CHECK

Similar rectangles have corresponding side lengths that are proportional. Use a proportion to check that rectangle *GHJK* is not similar to rectangle *PQRS*.

Practice

Each pair of figures below is similar. Identify the types of rigid and/or nonrigid motions that are needed to show this.

1.

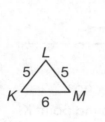

2.

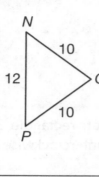

_____

_____

> **HINT** A dilation will be needed, since the figures are different sizes.

Identify the triangle that could be shown to be similar to △ABC if the sequence of motions described is performed.

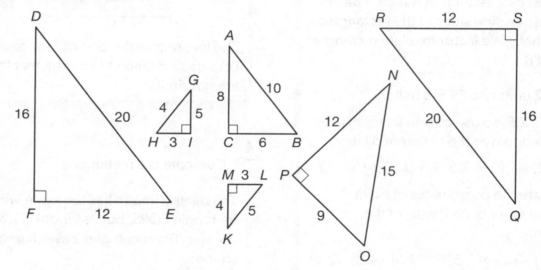

3. Triangle *ABC* is reflected across a horizontal line and then dilated by a scale factor of $\frac{1}{2}$.

_____

4. Triangle *ABC* is translated to the left and then dilated by a scale factor of 2.

_____

5. Triangle *ABC* is rotated 45° clockwise, translated to the right, and then dilated by a scale factor of 1.5.

_____

> **REMEMBER** A scale factor greater than 1 makes a figure larger.

Describe a sequence of rigid and nonrigid motions that could be used to show that each pair of figures is similar.

6.

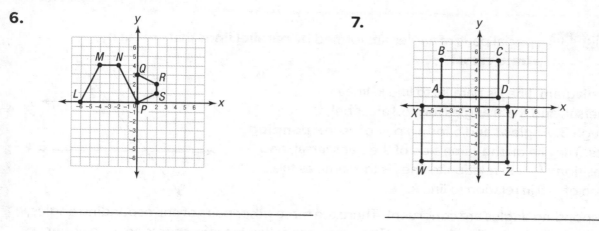

_____

_____

7.

_____

_____

Solve.

8. **DESCRIBE** Describe two different sequences of rigid and nonrigid motions that could be used to show that $\triangle BCD \sim \triangle DFG$. Explain why each sequence works.

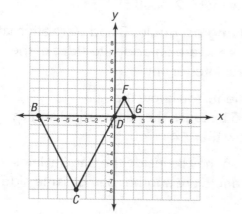

_____

9. **JUSTIFY** Is $\triangle JKL \sim \triangle PQR$? Use words and drawings to describe a sequence of rigid and nonrigid motions that justifies your answer.

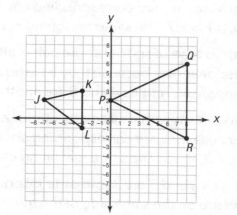

_____

Extending Understanding of Angle Relationships

LESSON 23

UNDERSTAND Special pairs of angles are formed by **parallel lines** that are cut by a **transversal**.

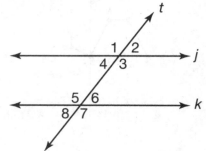

In the diagram, line *j* is parallel to line *k*, line *t* is a transversal, and the 8 angles formed are labeled 1 through 8. Angles 1 and 5 form a pair of **corresponding angles**. They lie on the same side of the transversal, and the position of ∠1 in relation to line *j* is the same as the position of ∠5 in relation to line *k*.

Corresponding angles are congruent. There are three other pairs of corresponding angles: ∠2 and ∠6; ∠3 and ∠7; ∠4 and ∠8. Therefore, the following statements are true about the angles shown in the diagram:

$$\angle 1 \cong \angle 5 \qquad \angle 3 \cong \angle 7$$
$$\angle 2 \cong \angle 6 \qquad \angle 4 \cong \angle 8$$

Another type of special angle pair is **alternate exterior angles**. Angles 1 and 7 are alternate exterior angles because they lie outside the parallel lines and are on opposite sides of the transversal. Angles 2 and 8 are another pair of alternate exterior angles.

You can show that alternate exterior angles are congruent. You know that ∠1 ≅ ∠5 because they are corresponding angles; and ∠5 ≅ ∠7 because they are **vertical angles**. So, ∠1 ≅ ∠7. The same reasoning can be used to show that ∠2 ≅ ∠8.

A third type of special angle pair is **alternate interior angles**. Angles 3 and 5 are alternate interior angles because they lie inside the parallel lines and are on opposite sides of the transversal. Angles 4 and 6 are another pair of alternate interior angles.

You can show that alternate interior angles are congruent. You know that ∠3 ≅ ∠7 because they are corresponding angles; and ∠7 ≅ ∠5 because they are vertical angles. So, ∠3 ≅ ∠5. The same reasoning can be used to show that ∠4 ≅ ∠6.

Angles 4 and 5 are **same-side interior angles** because they lie inside the parallel lines and are on the same side of the transversal. Angles 3 and 6 are another pair of same-side interior angles.

You can show that same-side interior angles are supplementary angles. Since adjacent angles 1 and 4 form a straight line, you know that m∠1 + m∠4 = 180°. Because angles 1 and 5 are corresponding angles, m∠1 = m∠5. Then, by substitution, m∠5 + m∠4 = 180°. So, angles 4 and 5 are supplementary. You can use the same reasoning to show that angles 3 and 6 are supplementary.

⊏ Connect

Line *m* ∥ line *n*. Both lines are cut by a transversal, line *l*.
If m∠4 = 114°, what are the measures of angles 1, 2, 3, 5, 6, 7, and 8? (The symbol ∥ means "is parallel to.")

1 Use what you know about same-side interior angles to find m∠5.

Same-side interior angles are supplementary, so m∠4 + m∠5 = 180°.

$$114° + m∠5 = 180°$$

$$m∠5 = 180° - 114° = 66°$$

2 Use what you know about corresponding angles to find the measures of ∠1 and ∠8.

Since angles 1 and 5 are corresponding angles, m∠1 = m∠5 = 66°.

Since angles 4 and 8 are corresponding angles, m∠4 = m∠8 = 114°.

3 Use what you know about alternate exterior angles to find the measures of angles 2 and 7.

Angles 2 and 8 are alternate exterior angles, so m∠2 = m∠8 = 114°.

Angles 1 and 7 are alternate exterior angles, so m∠7 = m∠1 = 66°.

4 Use what you know about alternate interior angles to find the measures of angles 3 and 6.

Angles 3 and 5 are alternate interior angles, so m∠3 = m∠5 = 66°.

Angles 4 and 6 are alternate interior angles, so m∠6 = m∠4 = 114°.

▶ Angles 1, 3, 5, and 7 measure 66°.
Angles 2, 4, 6, and 8 measure 114°.

GENERALIZE

Based on this example, make a generalization about the acute angles formed when two parallel lines are cut by a transversal. Then make a generalization about the obtuse angles.

Practice

Line _a_ ∥ line _b_. Both lines are cut by a transversal, line _c_. Identify each pair of angles as congruent or supplementary.

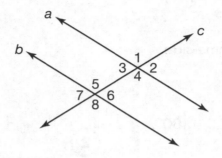

1. angles 1 and 5

_____

2. angles 2 and 7

_____

3. angles 3 and 5

_____

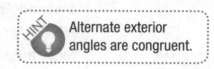

HINT Alternate exterior angles are congruent.

Line _x_ ∥ line _y_. Both lines are cut by a transversal, line _z_. Identify each pair of the following.

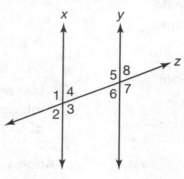

4. alternate interior angles

_____

_____

5. corresponding angles

_____

_____

6. alternate exterior angles

_____

_____

REMEMBER Corresponding angles lie on the same side of a transversal and on the same side of each parallel line.

Choose the best answer.

7. Lines *m* and *n* are parallel lines cut by a transversal, line *q*. Which of the following is **not** supplementary to ∠7?

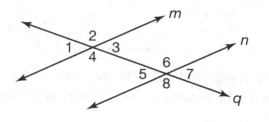

A. ∠3

B. ∠4

C. ∠6

D. ∠8

8. Line *a* ∥ line *b*. If they are cut by a transversal, line *t*, what is the value of *x*?

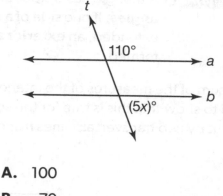

A. 100

B. 70

C. 22

D. 14

9. **DEDUCE** Parallel lines *k* and *l* are cut by a transversal, line *m*.

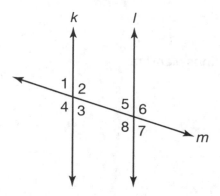

Yan knows that ∠1 and ∠5 are corresponding angles. She also knows that supplementary angles have measures that add to 180°. How could Yan use these two facts to deduce that ∠1 is supplementary to ∠6?

_____

_____

10. **EXPLAIN** A diagram of a barn door is shown. The two boards at the top and bottom are parallel. The measure of one 36° angle formed is given by the diagram.

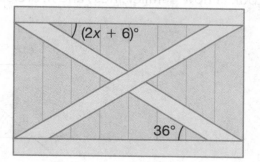

What is the value of *x*? Explain your reasoning and show your work.

_____

_____

Angles in Triangles

UNDERSTAND A triangle has 3 sides and 3 **interior angles**. If one side of a triangle is extended, an **exterior angle** is formed.

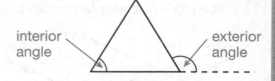

The sum of the measures of the interior angles in any triangle is 180°. This diagram can be used to show that this is true for the shaded triangle. In the diagram, line $l \parallel$ line m and they are cut by two transversals, lines n and p.

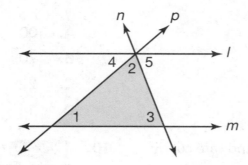

Adjacent angles 4, 2, and 5 form a straight line.

$m\angle 4 + m\angle 2 + m\angle 5 = 180°$

Look at how parallel lines l and m are cut by transversal lines n and p.

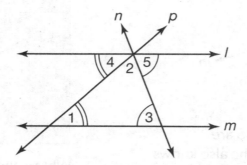

When line n cuts parallel lines l and m, it forms alternate interior angles 5 and 3.

Alternate interior angles are congruent, so $m\angle 5 = m\angle 3$.

When line p cuts parallel lines l and m, it forms alternate interior angles 4 and 1.

Alternate interior angles are congruent, so $m\angle 4 = m\angle 1$.

$m\angle 4 = m\angle 1$ and $m\angle 5 = m\angle 3$. Substitute $m\angle 1$ for $m\angle 4$ and $m\angle 3$ for $m\angle 5$ in the equation from above: $m\angle 4 + m\angle 2 + m\angle 5 = 180°$.

$m\angle 1 + m\angle 2 + m\angle 3 = 180°$

⊶ Connect

Find the value of x.

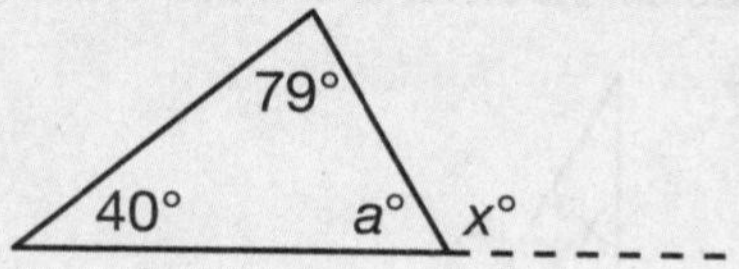

1 What does x represent?

It represents the degree measure of an exterior angle of the triangle.

2 First, find $a°$, the measure of the third interior angle of the triangle.

The sum of the measures of the interior angles of a triangle is 180°.

$$40° + 79° + a° = 180°$$
$$119° + a° = 180°$$
$$a° = 61°$$

3 Use the fact that the 61° interior angle and its exterior angle are supplementary to find the value of x.

$$61° + x° = 180°$$
$$x° = 119°$$
▶ $x = 119$

⟨**MODEL**⟩ Is the exterior angle in the example the only exterior angle that can be drawn for this triangle? If not, draw two others and label their measures $y°$ and $z°$.

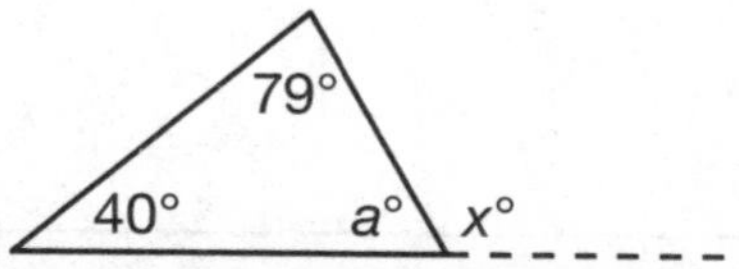

Practice

Write an equation that could be used to find the value of *x* for each triangle.

1.

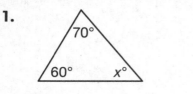

_____

2.

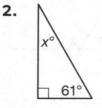

_____

3.

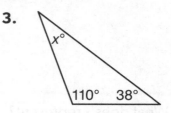

_____

> REMEMBER A right angle is 90°.

State whether or not it is possible to draw a triangle with the given interior angle measures.

4. 45°, 55°, 80°

_____

5. 30°, 60°, 100°

_____

6. 12°, 84°, 84°

_____

Find the value of *z* for each triangle. Show your work.

7.

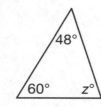

_____

8.

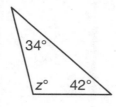

_____

9.

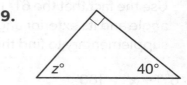

_____

Find the value of *x* for each triangle. Show your work.

10.

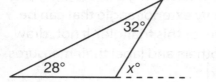

_____

11.

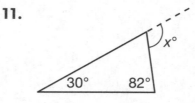

_____

12.

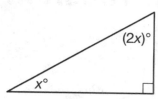

_____

13.

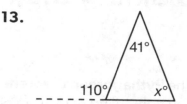

_____

Use the diagram below for questions 14–15.

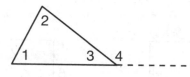

14. Why is this statement true?

$$m\angle 1 + m\angle 2 + m\angle 3 = 180°$$

_____

15. Why is this statement true?

$$m\angle 3 + m\angle 4 = 180°$$

_____

Solve.

16. **EXPLAIN** If two triangles have three pairs of corresponding angles that are congruent, the triangles must be similar. Would the information given in the diagram below be sufficient to allow you to prove that △ABC and △DEF are similar? Explain.

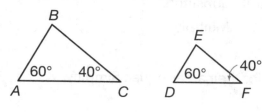

_____

_____

_____

17. **CONCLUDE** The triangle on the left has interior angles 1, 2, and 3.

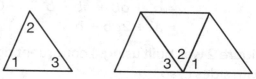

Marta copied this triangle 3 times, rotated those triangles, and placed them together so that angles 1, 2, and 3 were aligned. What does this allow you to conclude about the interior angle measures of a triangle? Explain.

_____

_____

_____

Explaining the Pythagorean Theorem

UNDERSTAND The **Pythagorean theorem** states that, in any right triangle, the sum of the squares of the lengths of the **legs** is equal to the square of the length of the **hypotenuse**.

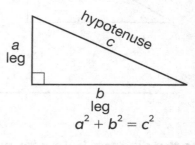

The two congruent squares shown below were built using congruent right triangles and squares with lengths a, b, and c. Use Figures 1 and 2 to prove the Pythagorean theorem.

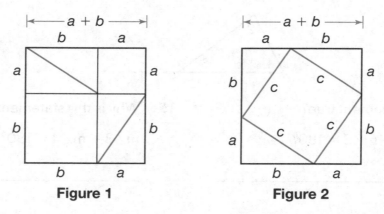

Figure 1   **Figure 2**

Let $(a + b)^2$, or $(a + b)(a + b)$, represent the area of Figure 1. Simplify.

A of Figure 1 $= (a + b)(a + b)$ Use the distributive property to simplify.
$\quad = (a)(a + b) + b(a + b)$
$\quad = a^2 + ab + ab + b^2$ Combine like terms.
$\quad = a^2 + 2ab + b^2$

Figure 2 was built using 4 congruent right triangles with base b and height a, and a square with sides c, so:

A of Figure 2 $= [4 \times (A \text{ of each triangle})] + (A \text{ of square})$ Substitute.
$\quad = \left(4 \times \frac{1}{2}ab\right) + c^2$ Multiply.
$\quad = 2ab + c^2$

Since the figures are congruent, set the expressions for their areas equal. Simplify.

$\quad (A \text{ of Figure 1}) = (A \text{ of Figure 2})$ Substitute.
$\quad a^2 + 2ab + b^2 = 2ab + c^2$ Subtract $2ab$ from both sides.
$a^2 + 2ab - 2ab + b^2 = 2ab - 2ab + c^2$
$\quad a^2 + b^2 = c^2$

The converse of the Pythagorean theorem states that if a triangle has sides of length a, b, and c such that $a^2 + b^2 = c^2$, then the triangle is a right triangle with a right angle opposite c.

⊸ᴇ Connect

Determine the length of $\overline{KL}$ in △JKL.

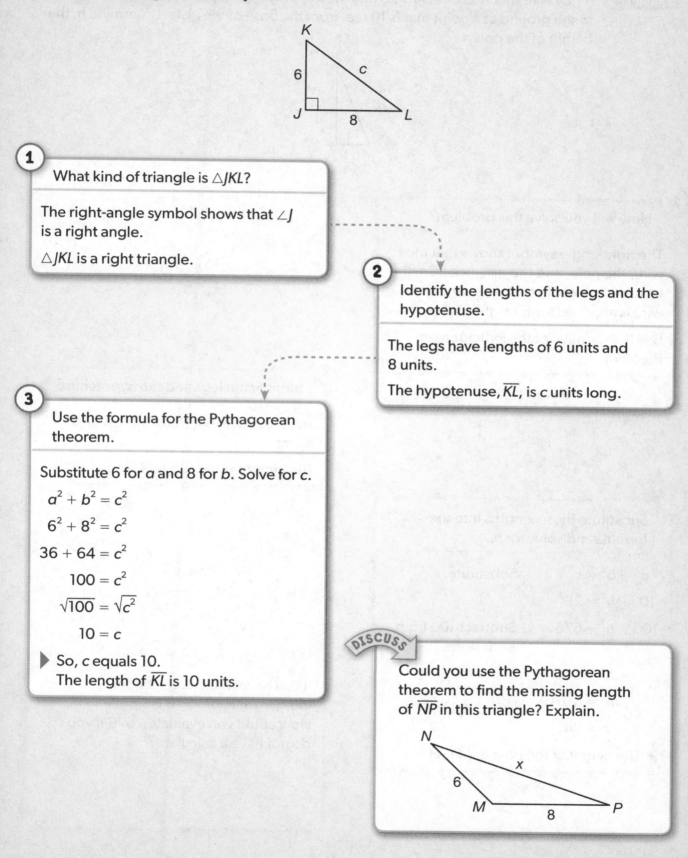

1 What kind of triangle is △JKL?

The right-angle symbol shows that ∠J is a right angle.

△JKL is a right triangle.

2 Identify the lengths of the legs and the hypotenuse.

The legs have lengths of 6 units and 8 units.

The hypotenuse, $\overline{KL}$, is c units long.

3 Use the formula for the Pythagorean theorem.

Substitute 6 for a and 8 for b. Solve for c.

$$a^2 + b^2 = c^2$$
$$6^2 + 8^2 = c^2$$
$$36 + 64 = c^2$$
$$100 = c^2$$
$$\sqrt{100} = \sqrt{c^2}$$
$$10 = c$$

▶ So, c equals 10.
The length of $\overline{KL}$ is 10 units.

DISCUSS Could you use the Pythagorean theorem to find the missing length of $\overline{NP}$ in this triangle? Explain.

A guy wire that is 26 feet long is attached to the top of a pole. The wire is attached to the ground at a point that is 10 feet from the base of the pole. Determine h, the height of the pole.

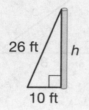

26 ft h

10 ft

1

How will you solve this problem?

The right-angle symbol shows that the wire, the pole, and the distance from the base of the pole to the place where the wire is attached form a right triangle.

Use the formula for the Pythagorean theorem.

2

Identify the legs and the hypotenuse.

The legs have lengths of 10 feet and h feet.

The hypotenuse is 26 feet long.

3

Substitute those lengths into the formula and solve for h.

$a^2 + b^2 = c^2$ Substitute.

$10^2 + h^2 = 26^2$

$100 + h^2 = 676$ Subtract 100 from both sides.

$h^2 = 576$

$\sqrt{h^2} = \sqrt{576}$

$h = 24$

▶ The height of the pole is 24 feet.

DISCUSS

If you have a calculator, finding the integer value of $\sqrt{576}$ is simple. How could you evaluate $\sqrt{576}$ if you do not have a calculator?

EXAMPLE B Rosa has three pencils, each a different length. The lengths are 18 centimeters, 15 centimeters, and 8 centimeters. Could she form a right triangle using these pencils as the sides?

1

What does the converse of the Pythagorean theorem state?

It states that if a triangle has side lengths a, b, and c such that $a^2 + b^2 = c^2$, then the triangle is a right triangle.

2

Identify the shorter pencil lengths and the longest pencil length.

The shorter lengths are 8 centimeters and 15 centimeters. Those would represent the shorter sides of the triangle. Let $a = 8$ and $b = 15$.

The longest length is 18 centimeters. Let $c = 18$.

3

Test the values in the formula.

$a^2 + b^2 = c^2$

$8^2 + 15^2 \stackrel{?}{=} 18^2$

$64 + 225 \stackrel{?}{=} 324$

$289 \neq 324$

8 centimeters, 15 centimeters, and 18 centimeters are not the side lengths of a right triangle.

▶ It is not possible for Rosa to use those pencils to make a right triangle.

TRY

Rosa finds that if she sharpens her longest pencil and shortens its length, she can use it to form a right triangle with the other two pencils. What length would she need to make the longest pencil?

Practice

Write an equation that shows the relationship between the given side lengths of these right triangles. Simplify if possible.

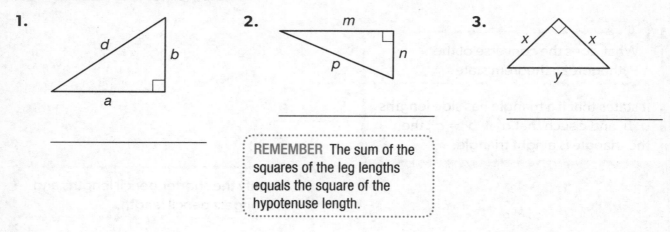

1.

_d_ _b_ _a_

_____

2.

_m_ _n_ _p_

_____

3.

_x_ _x_ _y_

_____

> REMEMBER The sum of the squares of the leg lengths equals the square of the hypotenuse length.

Use the converse of the Pythagorean theorem to determine whether or not a triangle with the given side lengths is a right triangle. Show your work.

4. 3 in., 4 in., 5 in.

_____

5. 4 yd, 7 yd, 11 yd

_____

6. 5 cm, 10 cm, 15 cm

_____

7. 9 cm, 39 cm, 41 cm

_____

8. 20 mm, 99 mm, 101 mm

_____

9. 4 m, 7.5 m, 8.5 m

_____

Choose the best answer.

10. A right triangle has legs measuring 15 meters and 20 meters. What is the length of the hypotenuse?

    A. 13 meters

    B. 17 meters

    C. 25 meters

    D. 35 meters

11. A right triangle has a leg measuring 24 units and a hypotenuse measuring 25 units. What is the length of the other leg?

    A. 7 units

    B. 9 units

    C. 35 units

    D. 49 units

Find x, the missing side length in each right triangle. Show your work.

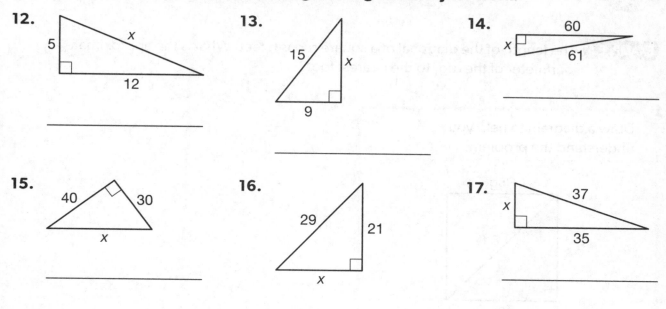

12.

5, x, 12

_____

13.

15, x, 9

_____

14.

60, x, 61

_____

15.

40, 30, x

_____

16.

29, 21, x

_____

17.

37, x, 35

_____

Prove. Use a centimeter ruler and a protractor, as needed.

18. **PROVE** Given: △FGH has sides a, b, and c units long, and it is true that $a^2 + b^2 = c^2$.

To prove that the converse of the Pythagorean theorem is true, show that △FGH is a right triangle.

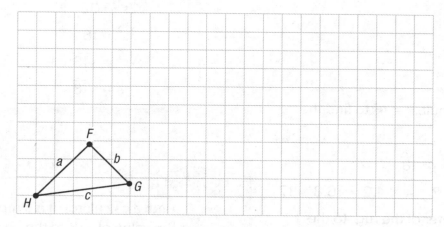

To do this, measure lengths a and b, in centimeters. Then draw a right triangle JKL, with legs a and b units long, and a hypotenuse labeled d. Make ∠J the right angle. Explain how you know that $a^2 + b^2 = d^2$. Then use a sequence of rigid motions to prove that △FGH is a right triangle. How does this show that △FGH is a right triangle?

_____

26 Applying the Pythagorean Theorem in Two and Three Dimensions

EXAMPLE A The length of the diagonal of a square rug is 6 feet. What is the approximate perimeter of the rug, to the nearest foot?

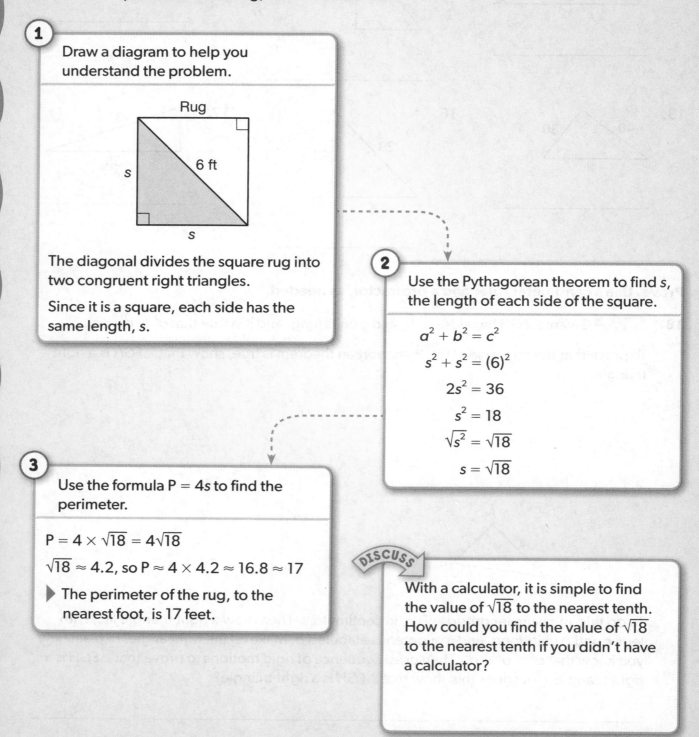

1

Draw a diagram to help you understand the problem.

Rug

6 ft

s

s

The diagonal divides the square rug into two congruent right triangles.

Since it is a square, each side has the same length, s.

2

Use the Pythagorean theorem to find s, the length of each side of the square.

$$a^2 + b^2 = c^2$$
$$s^2 + s^2 = (6)^2$$
$$2s^2 = 36$$
$$s^2 = 18$$
$$\sqrt{s^2} = \sqrt{18}$$
$$s = \sqrt{18}$$

3

Use the formula $P = 4s$ to find the perimeter.

$P = 4 \times \sqrt{18} = 4\sqrt{18}$

$\sqrt{18} \approx 4.2$, so $P \approx 4 \times 4.2 \approx 16.8 \approx 17$

▶ The perimeter of the rug, to the nearest foot, is 17 feet.

DISCUSS

With a calculator, it is simple to find the value of $\sqrt{18}$ to the nearest tenth. How could you find the value of $\sqrt{18}$ to the nearest tenth if you didn't have a calculator?

EXAMPLE B Javier has a suitcase, the inside of which is shaped like a rectangular prism with a length of 16 inches, a width of 12 inches, and a height of 7 inches. He wants to bring his largest umbrella, which is 21 inches in length, with him on a trip. Can he fit that umbrella in the suitcase?

1 Draw a mathematical diagram to help you understand the problem. (It does not need to look like a suitcase or an umbrella.)

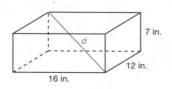

The rectangular prism represents the inside of the suitcase.

The space diagonal, d, represents the maximum length of an umbrella that could fit inside the suitcase.

2 Use the Pythagorean theorem to determine c, the length of the diagonal of the rectangular base of the prism, shown below.

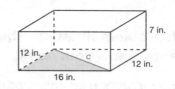

The diagonal divides the rectangular base into two right triangles, with legs 12 in. and 16 in., so:

$$a^2 + b^2 = c^2$$
$$12^2 + 16^2 = c^2$$
$$144 + 256 = c^2$$
$$400 = c^2$$
$$20 = c$$

3 The space diagonal, d, forms a right triangle with the diagonal of the base (20 in.) and the height of the prism (7 in.). Use the Pythagorean theorem to solve for d.

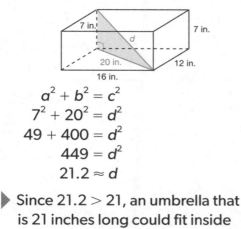

$$a^2 + b^2 = c^2$$
$$7^2 + 20^2 = d^2$$
$$49 + 400 = d^2$$
$$449 = d^2$$
$$21.2 \approx d$$

▶ Since 21.2 > 21, an umbrella that is 21 inches long could fit inside Javier's suitcase.

DISCUSS

If you didn't have a calculator, would you have needed to estimate the value of $\sqrt{449}$ to the nearest tenth in order to solve the problem on the page? Explain.

Practice

For each diagram, write an equation showing how the Pythagorean theorem could be used to find the value of x.

1.

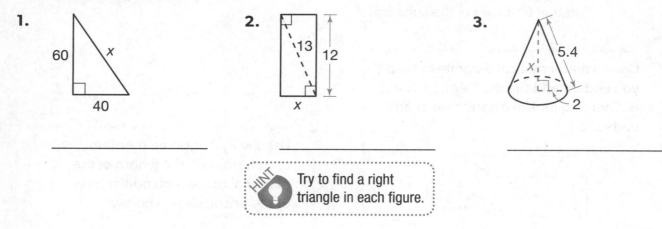

2.

3.

_____   _____   _____

> **HINT** Try to find a right triangle in each figure.

Read each problem situation. Then find the missing length, x. If necessary, round to the nearest tenth. Show your work.

4. A land surveyor uses this diagram to find x, the length of a lake.

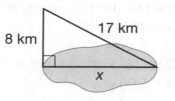

$x =$ _____

5. A 22-foot ladder leans against a shed, reaching a height of x feet. The base of the ladder is 10 feet from the shed.

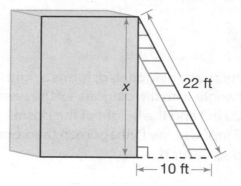

$x \approx$ _____

> **HINT** Is x the length of a leg or a hypotenuse?

Choose the best answer.

6. The diagram shows a sailboat. What is the approximate area of the sail shown?

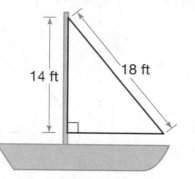

14 ft   18 ft

A. 79 square feet

B. 126 square feet

C. 158 square feet

D. 200 square feet

7. This television screen has a 25-inch diagonal and a 15-inch height. What is the area of the screen?

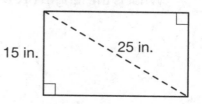

15 in.   25 in.

A. 150 square inches

B. 300 square inches

C. 375 square inches

D. 437 square inches

Solve.

8. EXPLAIN If two forces, *A* and *B*, pull at right angles from each other, the resultant force can be represented as the diagonal of a rectangle.

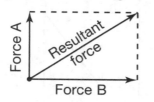

Force A   Resultant force   Force B

If a 21-pound force and a 28-pound force are pulling on an object, and the resultant force is 35 pounds, are the forces pulling at right angles? Explain.

_____

_____

9. JUSTIFY Lily has a storage box shaped like a rectangular prism with a length of 4 feet, a width of 3 feet, and a height of 2 feet. She has a fishing pole that is 6 feet long. Can she store the fishing pole in the box? Use words, numbers, and/or diagrams to justify your answer.

_____

_____

LESSON 27 Applying the Pythagorean Theorem on the Coordinate Plane

EXAMPLE A Line segment *CD* is plotted on the coordinate plane. What is the length of $\overline{CD}$?

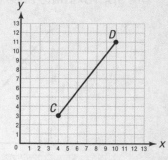

1

Identify the coordinates of each endpoint.

Point *C* is at (4, 3). Point *D* is at (10, 11).

2

How can you find the length of the line segment?

The line segment is not horizontal or vertical, so finding the length is not as simple as counting units or subtracting coordinates. However, line segment *CD* can become the hypotenuse of a right triangle, with one horizontal leg and one vertical leg, as shown.

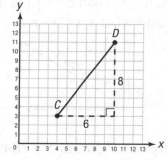

Now you can count units or subtract coordinates to find the lengths of the legs.

The horizontal leg connects (4, 3) to (10, 3), so subtract the *x*-coordinates.

Its length is $10 - 4 = 6$ units.

The vertical leg connects (10, 3) to (10, 11), so subtract the *y*-coordinates.

Its length is $11 - 3 = 8$ units.

3

Apply the Pythagorean theorem.

$$a^2 + b^2 = c^2$$
$$6^2 + 8^2 = c^2$$
$$36 + 64 = c^2$$
$$100 = c^2$$
$$10 = c$$

▶ The length of $\overline{CD}$ is 10 units.

MODEL

Show another way to draw the right triangle for this problem.

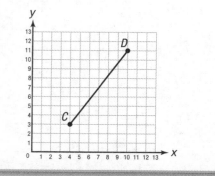

EXAMPLE B What is the distance between points *R* and *S*?

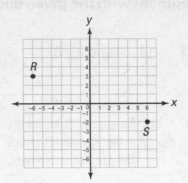

1

How can you find the length of the line segment?

Connect points *R* and *S* to form the hypotenuse of a right triangle.

Then draw horizontal and vertical legs, as shown.

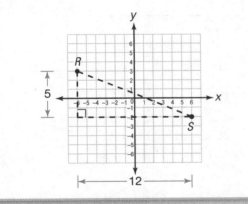

2

Apply the Pythagorean theorem.

$$a^2 + b^2 = c^2$$
$$5^2 + 12^2 = c^2$$
$$25 + 144 = c^2$$
$$169 = c^2$$
$$13 = c$$

▶ The distance between points *R* and *S* is 13 units.

TRY

What is the distance between points *T* and *V*? Estimate your answer to the nearest tenth.

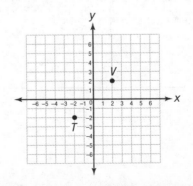

Practice

Determine the length of a line segment with the given endpoints. Use *Math Tool:*
Coordinate Plane.

1. (0, 7) and (0, 1)

2. (4, 8) and (6, 8)

3. (−1, 12) and (−1, 7)

_____

_____

_____

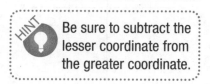

HINT

Be sure to subtract the
lesser coordinate from
the greater coordinate.

Determine the length of each line segment. Show your work.

4.

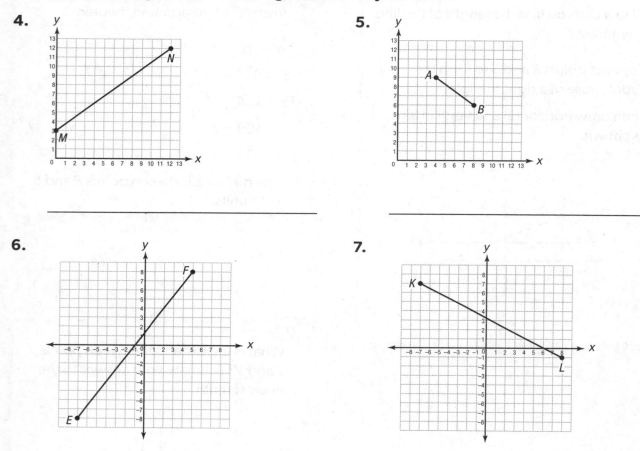

_____

5.

_____

6.

_____

7.

_____

On the town map at right, each unit represents 1 kilometer. Use the town map to answer questions 8 and 9.

8. Maksim jogs directly from City Hall to the public library. How many kilometers does he jog? Show your work.

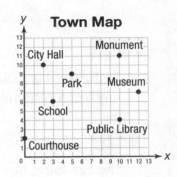

_____

9. A crow flies directly from the courthouse to the museum. What distance does the crow fly? Show your work.

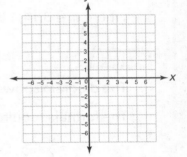

_____

Plot the points on the coordinate plane. Then calculate the distance between the two points. Round your answer to the nearest tenth. Show your work.

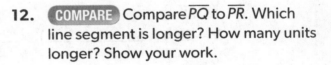

10. point $V(-5, 2)$ and point $W(1, -2)$

_____

Solve.

11. **DRAW** Draw a diagonal for rectangle ABCD and calculate its length. Is it possible to draw a different diagonal for this rectangle that has a different length? Explain.

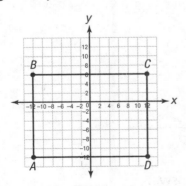

_____

12. **COMPARE** Compare $\overline{PQ}$ to $\overline{PR}$. Which line segment is longer? How many units longer? Show your work.

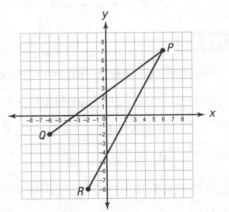

_____

LESSON 28 — Problem Solving: Volume

Soup Can

READ

To the right is a diagram of a soup can. To the nearest tenth of a centimeter, what is the volume of the can?

|← 8 cm →|

POTATO SOUP

10 cm

PLAN

The can looks like a _____, so use that volume formula.

From *Math Tool: Volume Formulas:*

$$V = \pi r^2 h,$$

where $\pi \approx 3.14$, r is the radius, and h is the height.

SOLVE

The diagram shows that the diameter is 8 cm. The height is _____ cm.

The formula requires the radius, and the radius is half the diameter.

$$r = \frac{d}{2} = \frac{8}{2} = \text{_____ cm}$$

Substitute and simplify.

$$V = \pi r^2 h$$

$$V \approx 3.14 \times (\text{_____})^2 \times \text{_____}$$

$$V \approx \text{_____}$$

CHECK

Estimate to check that your answer is reasonable.

For example, use 3 instead of 3.14 for π.

$$V \approx 3 \times (\text{_____})^2 \times \text{_____}$$

$$V \approx \text{_____}$$

Is that estimate close to your answer?

That estimate is _____ to my answer, so my answer _____ reasonable.

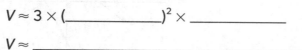 The approximate volume of the soup can is _____ cubic centimeters.

Carnival Treats

READ

At the school carnival, popcorn is given out in paper treat cones, like the one shown to the right. Approximately how many cubic inches can each cone hold?

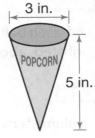

3 in.

POPCORN

5 in.

PLAN

The shape is given. It is a cone.

Volume is measured in cubic units, so use the formula for finding the volume of a _____.

From *Math Tool: Volume Formulas:*

$$V = \frac{1}{3}\pi r^2 h,$$

where $\pi \approx 3.14$, r is the radius, and h is the height.

SOLVE

The diagram shows that the height is 5 inches and the diameter is 3 inches.

The formula requires the radius, and the radius is _____ the diameter.

$$r = \underline{\hspace{4cm}}$$

Substitute and simplify.

$$V = \frac{1}{3}\pi r^2 h$$

$$V \approx \frac{1}{3} \times 3.14 \times (\underline{\hspace{2cm}})^2 \times 5$$

$$V \approx \underline{\hspace{6cm}}$$

CHECK

Check that you answered the question that was asked.

The question asked you to determine approximately how many cubic inches each cone can hold.

Is your answer in cubic inches? _____

Did you use an approximation for π? _____

▶ The cone can hold approximately _____ cubic inches.

Beach Ball

READ

A beach ball has a diameter of 14 inches. If the beach ball is fully inflated, about how many cubic inches of air will it hold?

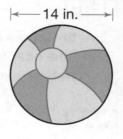

|← 14 in. →|

PLAN

Volume is measured in cubic units, so use the formula for finding the volume of a _____.

From *Math Tool: Volume Formulas*:

$$V = \frac{4}{3}\pi r^3,$$

where $\pi \approx 3.14$ and r is the radius.

SOLVE

The diagram shows that the _____ is 14 inches.

The formula requires the radius, and the radius is $\frac{1}{2}$ the _____.

$$r = \underline{\hspace{5cm}}$$

Since the radius is _____, using $\frac{22}{7}$ for π will make the computation simpler.

Substitute and simplify.

$$V = \frac{4}{3}\pi r^3$$
$$V \approx \frac{4}{3} \times \frac{22}{7} \times (\boxed{})^3$$
$$V \approx \underline{\hspace{6cm}}$$

CHECK

Estimate to check that your answer is reasonable.

Even though you didn't use 3.14 for π, you can still use 3 for π to check your answer.

$$V \approx \frac{4}{3} \times 3 \times (\underline{\hspace{3cm}})^3$$
$$V \approx \underline{\hspace{6cm}}$$

Is that estimate close to your answer?

That estimate is _____ to my answer, so my answer _____ reasonable.

▶ The fully inflated beach ball will hold about _____ cubic inches of air.

Tennis Balls in a Can

READ

A cylindrical can holds three tennis balls snugly, one directly above another. If the radius of a tennis ball is 3.4 centimeters, what volume of the can is occupied by the air outside the tennis balls?

PLAN

The diagram shows 3 spheres inside a cylinder.

So, use the formula for finding the volume of a sphere, which is $V = \frac{4}{3}\pi r^3$.

You will also use the formula for finding the volume of a cylinder, which is:

$V =$ _____

The height will equal 3 diameters, or _____ times 3.4 cm. To find the air that is inside the cylinder, but outside the tennis balls, subtract the combined volume of the 3 _____ from the volume of the cylinder.

SOLVE

Find the volume of one tennis ball, in terms of π.

$V = \frac{4}{3} \times \pi \times (3.4)^3$

$V \approx$ _____ π cm^3

Find the height of the cylinder: $h = 6r = 6 \times 3.4 =$ _____ cm

Substitute that and other values into the formula for finding the volume of a cylinder. Find the volume in terms of π.

$V =$ _____

$V \approx$ _____ π cm^3

Subtract to find the volume you need.

$V = $ (volume of cylinder) $-$ (3 $\times$ volume of one tennis ball)

$V \approx$ _____ π cm^3

CHECK

Use *Math Tool: Volume Formulas*. Are the formulas you used correct? _____

▶ The volume of the can that is occupied by the air outside the tennis balls is about _____ cubic centimeters.

Practice

Use the 4-step problem-solving process to solve each problem.

1. **READ**   Erika bought a plastic run-around ball for her guinea pig.

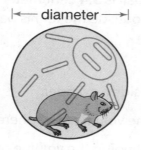

$\longleftarrow$ diameter $\longrightarrow$

If the volume of the ball is 288π cubic inches, what is the diameter of the ball?

PLAN   _____

_____

SOLVE

CHECK

2. About how many cubic meters of water will this swimming pool hold if it is filled to capacity?

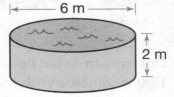

3. A cone-shaped paper water cup has a radius of 4 centimeters and a volume of 48π cubic centimeters. What is the height of the cup?

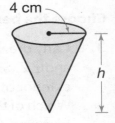

4. A silo of a barn consists of a cylinder capped by a hemisphere (half-sphere). The height of the cylinder is 60 feet and its diameter is 30 feet. What is the approximate volume of the silo?

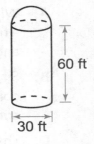

Review

Describe in detail how one or more rigid motions could be used to make the leftmost figure coincide with the rightmost figure. Use the least number of rigid motions possible.

1.

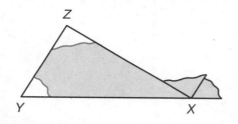

_____

_____

2.

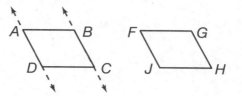

_____

_____

Choose the best answer.

3. Carly drew triangle *XYZ* and tore off ∠*Y* and ∠*Z*. She then fit the angles on the exterior of the third angle, as shown. Which of the following facts about triangles does this demonstrate?

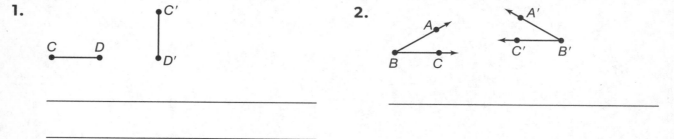

A. When parallel lines are cut by a transversal, alternate interior angles are congruent.

B. Similar triangles have corresponding angles that are congruent.

C. The sum of the squares of the lengths of the legs is equal to the square of the length of the hypotenuse.

D. The sum of the measures of the interior angles of a triangle is 180°.

4. Parallelogram *ABCD* will be translated to the right so that it coincides with parallelogram *FGHJ*. Which statement will be true of lines *AD* and *BC* which contain $\overline{AD}$ and $\overline{BC}$ on this parallelogram?

A. Parallel lines *AD* and *BC* will move onto parallel lines *FG* and *HJ*, which contain $\overline{FG}$ and $\overline{HJ}$.

B. Parallel lines *AD* and *BC* will move onto parallel lines *FJ* and *GH*, which contain $\overline{FJ}$ and $\overline{GH}$.

C. Parallel lines *AB* and *CD* will be turned differently after the translation.

D. Parallel lines *AB* and *CD* will be mirror images of one another after the translation.

Use the converse of the Pythagorean theorem to determine whether or not a triangle with the given side lengths is a right triangle. Show your work.

5. 30 in., 40 in., 50 in.

6. 3 yd, 4 yd, 6 yd

7. 11 cm, 60 cm, 61 cm

_____   _____   _____

Choose the best answer.

8. Lines *m* and *n* are parallel lines cut by a transversal, line *t*. Which of the following angles is **not** congruent to ∠3?

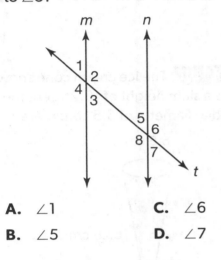

A. ∠1

B. ∠5

C. ∠6

D. ∠7

9. A fire truck is parked so the base of its ladder is 15 feet from a building and 10 feet above the ground. The ladder extends to a length of 20 feet. Based on the diagram, approximately how high on the building does the ladder reach?

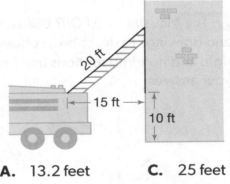

A. 13.2 feet

B. 23.2 feet

C. 25 feet

D. 35 feet

10. Which sequence could be used to show that the triangles are congruent?

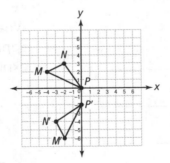

A. 90°-clockwise rotation of △MNP around the origin, followed by a translation to the left

B. 90°-counterclockwise rotation of △MNP around the origin, followed by a translation to the left

C. 90°-clockwise rotation of △MNP around the origin, followed by a translation down

D. 90°-counterclockwise rotation of △MNP around the origin, followed by a translation down

Find the length of each line segment.

11.

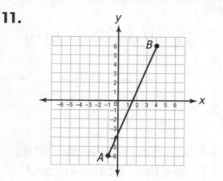

_____

12.

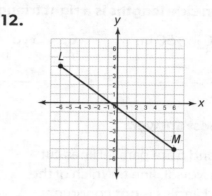

_____

Solve.

13. (JUSTIFY) Is △JKL ~ △PQR? Use words and drawings to describe a sequence of rigid and nonrigid motions that justifies your answer.

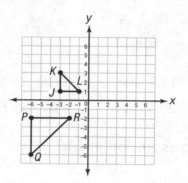

_____

_____

_____

_____

_____

_____

14. (COMPUTE) The ice cream cone shown has a slant height of 15.25 centimeters and a diameter of 5.5 centimeters.

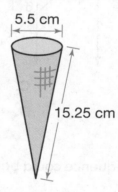

What is its height? What is its approximate volume? Show and explain your work.

_____

_____

PROVING THE PYTHAGOREAN THEOREM

Working in small groups or individually, use *Math Tool: Pythagorean Theorem Proof* to help informally prove the Pythagorean Theorem.

1. On the Math Tool page, you will see a right triangle with sides labeled a, b, and c on grid paper. You will also see that lengths for a, b, and c are given. Use those lengths and the grid paper to draw the following:

   - square with sides a units long
   - square with sides b units long
   - square with sides c units long

Write the area of each square in its center. For example, for the square with sides a units long, the area, a^2, should be written in its center.

2. Shade or color each square so each looks different than the others. Then cut out the right triangle with sides a, b, and c, and the squares that you drew on the grid paper. Place each square against the appropriate side of the right triangle, like this. ➡️

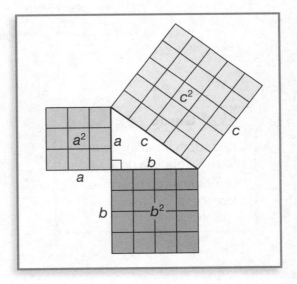

3. Now, show that the combined area of the two smaller squares $(a^2 + b^2)$ is equal to the area of the largest square (c^2). To do this, place the smaller squares on top of the largest square until it is completely covered. You will need to cut up one of the squares in order to completely cover the largest square with no gaps or overlaps.

4. What is the formula for the Pythagorean Theorem? How did you just prove that it is true?

_____

_____

_____

_____

Grade 7 RP

Analyze proportional relationships and use them to solve real-world and mathematical problems.

Grade 8 SP

Investigate patterns of association in bivariate data.

Grade 7 SP

Use random sampling to draw inferences about a population. Draw informal comparative inferences about two populations.

Domain 5
Statistics and Probability

LESSON 29

Constructing and Interpreting Scatter Plots

UNDERSTAND The numbers of years of work experience of 14 employees makes up a set of numerical data. The hourly wages of those 14 employees also makes up a set of numerical data. If the years of experience and hourly wage of each employee are linked, those ordered pairs of data are called **bivariate data**. Bivariate data is often displayed in a **scatter plot**. A scatter plot can help you determine if there is a relationship, or association, between pairs of data.

To determine if an association exists, look at the points on a scatter plot to see if they cluster in a band or are randomly scattered. If one data point is very different from the others, you do not need to consider it when looking for an association. That point is called an **outlier**.

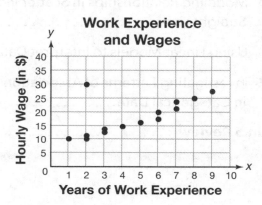

Using the scatter plot above, describe the association, if any, that exists between years of experience and hourly wage.

The first step is to decide if the data points cluster in a straight or curved band, or if they look randomly scattered.

Except for the outlier at (2, 30), the pattern of data points appears to cluster in a straight band. This means there is a strong, linear association.

Now you can describe the association.

The data points slant up from left to right. So, as *x*-values increase, *y*-values also tend to increase. This means the association is positive.

The scatter plot shows a strong, positive linear association. It shows that hourly wages increase with years of experience.

⊱ Connect

The owner of a diner wanted to find out if outside temperature affects soup sales. The table and scatter plot show a sample of data that the owner collected.

Temperature (in °F)	30	32	35	40	40	45	54	60	64	68
Bowls of Soup Sold	8	50	42	42	38	28	22	15	16	5

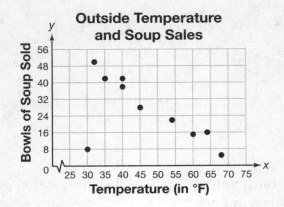

Is there an association between the outside temperature and soup sales? If so, did you exclude any outliers when determining that association?

1

Decide if the data points cluster in a straight or curved band, or if they look randomly scattered.

Except for the outlier at (30, 8), the pattern of data points appears to cluster in a straight band. This means there is a strong, linear association.

2

Describe the association.

The data points slant down from left to right. So, as x-values increase, y-values tend to decrease. This means the association is negative.

▶ The scatter plot shows a strong, negative linear association. As the temperature increases, the number of bowls of soup sold decreases.

DISCUSS

How can you determine the sign of the slope of a line from looking at its graph? Explain how this knowledge can help you identify a positive or negative linear association on a scatter plot.

Practice

For each scatter plot, describe the association shown as linear or nonlinear. If no association is shown, state that. If the association is linear, identify it as positive or negative.

1.
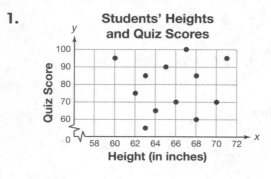

2.
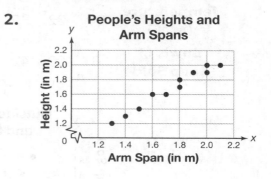

_____

Choose the best answer.

3. The scatter plot shows the lengths of several babies and the numbers representing the months in which they were born. Which best describes the association, if any, that is shown?

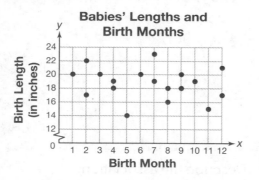

A. positive association

B. negative association

C. no association

D. nonlinear association

4. The scatter plot shows the ages of appliances and the costs of repairing them. Which best describes the association, if any, that is shown?

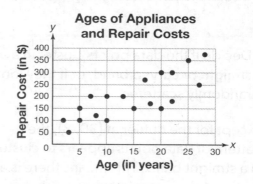

A. positive association

B. negative association

C. no association

D. nonlinear association

Fill in the blanks.

5. Bivariate data refers to _____ of linked numerical observations.

6. If data in a scatter plot form a straight band, the plot shows _____ association.

7. If data in a scatter plot are randomly scattered, the plot shows _____ association.

Describe the association shown, if any, by the scatter plot in as many ways as possible, using terms such as linear or nonlinear and positive or negative. Identify any outlier(s).

8.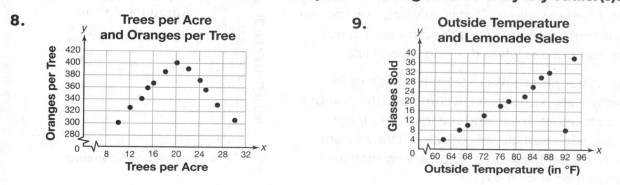

9.

Solve.

10. CREATE The table shows the numbers of minutes 10 shoppers spent in a supermarket and the total amount each spent during that shopping trip. On the grid below, create a scatter plot using the data in the table. Then describe the association shown, if any, in as many ways as possible. Identify any outlier(s).

Time and Total Spent

Time (in min)	Total (in USD)
10	$20
30	$80
50	$120
20	$40
60	$150
30	$60
40	$90
70	$180
60	$20
50	$140

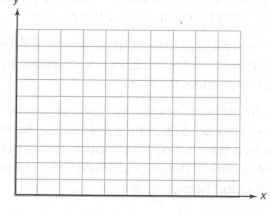

Modeling Relationships in Scatter Plots with Straight Lines

LESSON 30

UNDERSTAND If the data points on a scatter plot show a linear association, you can draw a straight line that models the general trend of the data. This **line of best fit**, or **trend line**, will probably not fit all the data points exactly. However, if the line you draw is a good fit, it will be close to most of the data points.

Any point on a trend line will be representative of the data set values. That is, any point on the line would not be an outlier for the data set. Do not consider outliers when drawing a trend line.

The scatter plot shows data for a sample of 14 charity-walk participants. It compares the number of sponsors each had and the total amount of money each participant collected. Draw a trend line to model these data. Explain why that line is a good model for the data.

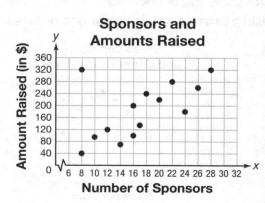

The first step is to describe the association shown on the scatter plot.

Excluding the outlier at (8, 320), the pattern of data points shows a positive, linear association. As the number of sponsors increased, the total amount of money collected increased. The line of best fit will have a positive slope.

Then draw a line that fits the data points well. Try to draw a line with about as many points above it as below it. Ignore the outlier.

The trend line is a good fit for the data if there are about the same number of points above the line as there are below the line.

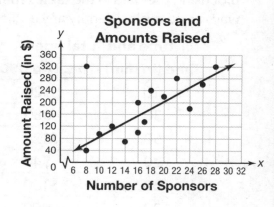

The trend line is shown in the graph to the right. There are about as many data points above the line as below it. So, even though the line does not contain any of the data points on the scatter plot, it is a good fit for the data.

⊸€ Connect

This scatter plot compares the number of pages in several novels in the school library to the number of times the novels were checked out last year.

Draw a trend line for these data and explain why it is a good fit for the data. Is the line you drew the only possible trend line that could be drawn for these data?

1 Describe the association shown on the scatter plot.

Excluding the outlier at (400, 18), the pattern of data points shows a negative, linear association. This means that the line of best fit will have a negative slope.

2 Draw a line that fits the data points well.

Try to draw a line with about as many points above it as below it. Ignore the outlier.

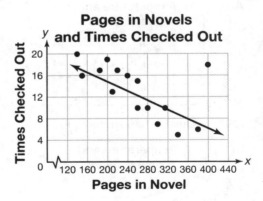

The trend line shows that books with fewer pages were checked out of the library more frequently, and books with more pages were checked out less frequently.

3 Is the line you drew the only possible trend line for these data?

▶ No, there is no one exact line that fits the data perfectly, so it is possible to draw a slightly different line that is still close to most of the data points. One trend line is shown in the figure to the right. It has about the same number of points above it as below it.

DISCUSS

Based on the trend line, would you expect a 360-page novel to have been checked out 20 times? Explain.

Practice

Describe the association shown by the scatter plot and explain why the trend line shown for each scatter plot is a good fit for the data.

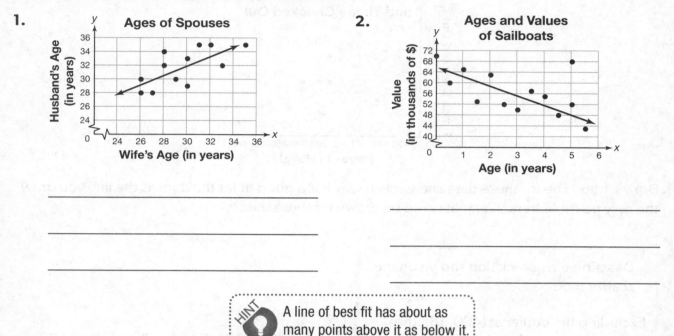

1. **Ages of Spouses**

2. **Ages and Values of Sailboats**

_____

_____

_____

_____

_____

_____

> **HINT** A line of best fit has about as many points above it as below it.

Consider each pair of identical scatter plots. Circle the letter of the plot that shows the better trend line. Explain your choice.

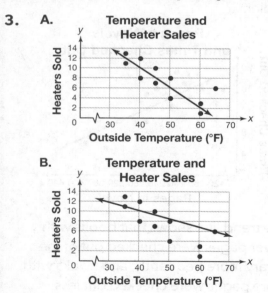

3. A. **Temperature and Heater Sales**

B. **Temperature and Heater Sales**

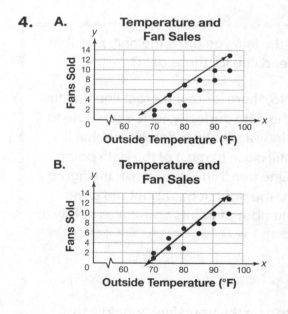

4. A. **Temperature and Fan Sales**

B. **Temperature and Fan Sales**

_____

_____

_____

_____

Write true or false for each statement. If false, rewrite the statement so it is true.

5. A straight line is a good model for a scatter plot that shows a nonlinear association.

_____

6. A trend line should always pass through at least two actual data points on a scatter plot.

_____

7. A trend line will never include a point that is an outlier for a data set.

_____

Solve.

8. `DRAW` The scatter plot shows the numbers of times different popular movies were rented and the number of weeks since the release of each movie.

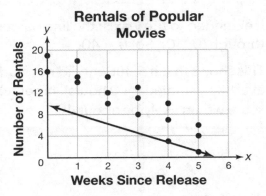

Is the line drawn a good model for the data? If not, draw a better model. Explain.

_____

_____

9. `EXPLAIN` The scatter plot shows the heights and weights of players on a professional basketball team. Draw a line of best fit for the data.

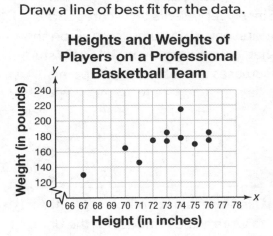

Based on your line, would you expect a professional basketball player who is 77 inches tall to weigh 140 pounds? Explain.

_____

_____

31 Using Linear Models to Interpret Data

EXAMPLE A Ms. Jones collected data from a sample of 14 students to determine the association between the numbers of hours they studied for a test and their test scores. She created this scatter plot to show her data. The line shows the general trend of the data.

Write an equation for the linear model. Explain what the slope and y-intercept represent in this situation.

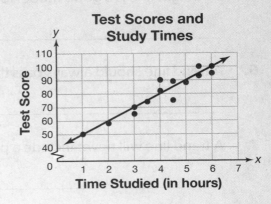

Test Scores and Study Times

1 Identify the slope, m.

The line passes through (1, 50) and (6, 100).

$$m = \frac{\text{change in } y}{\text{change in } x} = \frac{100 - 50}{6 - 1} = \frac{50}{5} = 10$$

Since y represents test scores and x represents study times, the slope shows that, on average, every 1 hour of study increases a test score by 10 points.

2 Identify the y-intercept, b.

If extended to the y-axis, the line passes through (0, 40). So, b = 40.

This shows that if a student did not study at all (i.e., studied for 0 hours), his or her score would likely be about 40.

3 Use slope-intercept form, y = mx + b, to write a linear model for the data.

Substitute 10 for m and 40 for b.

▶ The linear model is y = 10x + 40. According to the model, a student who does not study at all is likely to score 40 points. However, for each hour a student studies, this score is likely to increase by 10 points.

DISCUSS

Explain why the linear model shown is not a perfect predictor of the score a student will receive if he or she studies for a certain number of hours.

EXAMPLE B Custom Company makes custom T-shirts. The cost per T-shirt varies, depending on the design chosen and the number of T-shirts ordered. The scatter plot below shows a sample of T-shirt orders.

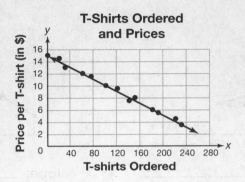

T-Shirts Ordered and Prices

Write an equation for the linear model. Interpret the slope and y-intercept of this model.

1 Identify the slope, *m*.

The line passes through (0, 15) and (240, 3).

$$m = \frac{\text{change in } y}{\text{change in } x} = \frac{3-15}{240-0} = -\frac{12}{240} = -0.05$$

Since *y* represents the price per T-shirt and *x* represents the number of shirts ordered, the slope shows that, on average, the cost per shirt decreases by $0.05 with each additional shirt ordered.

2 Identify the y-intercept, *b*.

The line passes through (0, 15). So, *b* = 15.

This shows that the cost per T-shirt will be less than $15, no matter how many are ordered.

3 Use the slope-intercept form, *y* = *mx* + *b*, to write a linear model.

▶ The linear model is *y* = −0.05*x* + 15. According to the model, no shirts would be sold if the price were $15, and the price per T-shirt decreases by about $0.05 with each additional shirt sold.

TRY A competitor, T-Shirt Town, uses the model *y* = −0.10*x* + 15 to determine *y*, the cost if *x* T-shirts are ordered. Compare the slope and y-intercept for this model to that of the company in the example. Which company offers the better deal?

Practice

Identify the slope and y-intercept for each linear model given.

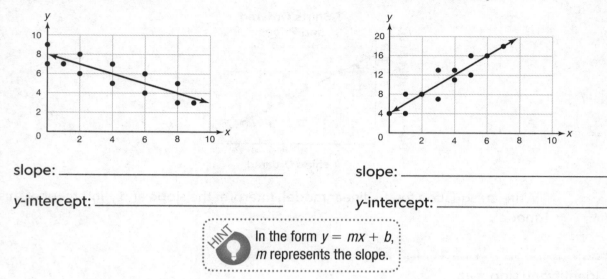

1. The linear model is $y = -0.5x + 8$.

slope: _____

y-intercept: _____

2. The linear model is $y = 2x + 4$.

slope: _____

y-intercept: _____

> HINT
> In the form $y = mx + b$,
> m represents the slope.

Choose the best answer.

3. The scatter plot shows the numbers of hours that students spent using social media the night before a test, and their test scores. The data is modeled by the function $y = -8x + 100$. Which is the best interpretation of the y-intercept of this model?

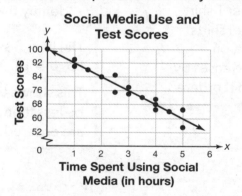

A. The use of social media the night before a test does not affect a student's score.

B. Students who use social media for 8 hours the night before are most likely to score 100.

C. Students who use social media for 0 hours the night before are most likely to score 100.

D. Using social media for 100 hours the night before lowers a student's score by 0 points.

Identify the slope and *y*-intercept for each model. Then tell what each represents in the problem.

4. The scatter plot shows the number of years since a new science initiative for girls was started and the number of girls enrolled in science classes at several high schools. The data is modeled by the function $y = 25x + 150$.

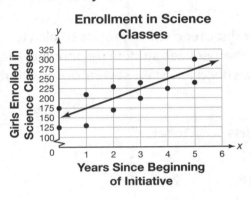

5. The scatter plot shows the number of months since a family purchased a treadmill and the number of hours each family member used it each month. The data is modeled by the function $y = -4x + 24$.

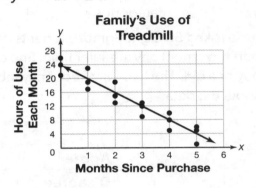

Solve.

6. **INTERPRET** The scatter plot shows the number of minutes that Jayson played during a basketball game and the number of points he scored. The data is modeled by the function $y = \frac{1}{3}x + 1$.

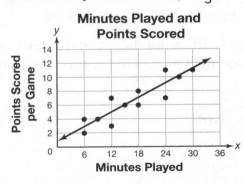

Interpret the slope and *y*-intercept of the model. Describe the limitations of this model in predicting how many points Jayson might score during an actual game.

7. **EXPLAIN** A company sells laptops to small businesses. The cost per laptop varies, depending on the model selected and the number ordered. The scatter plot shows a sample of laptop orders.

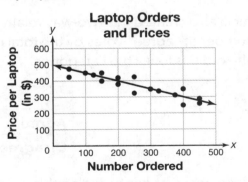

Write an equation for the linear model. Show or explain your work. Then interpret the slope of the model.

Investigating Patterns of Association in Categorical Data

UNDERSTAND If the data you collect is a set of numbers, you are collecting numerical data. If instead you collect data about the categories or groups to which people or objects belong, you are collecting categorical data. A two-way **frequency** table is one way to display bivariate categorical data. It shows the total number of data points that fall into different categories.

Lucia asked 50 eighth-grade students if they agreed or disagreed with a proposed plan to start the school day at a later time. She also recorded whether each student responding was a boy or a girl. The two-way frequency table below shows her data. Make several observations about the data.

	Boys	**Girls**	**Total**
Agree	14	12	26
Disagree	6	18	24
Total	20	30	50

Look at the data. What do you notice?

▶ There were 20 boys and 30 girls surveyed, so more girls were surveyed than boys. The total number of "agree" and "disagree" votes was about the same; however, more girls than boys disagreed.

These same data could also be displayed as percents in a two-way **relative frequency** table. The relative frequency for a given category is found by dividing the frequency for that category by the sum of all frequencies. So, a relative frequency table shows percents.

Lucia also created this two-way relative frequency table to show her data. She divided the number of "agree" votes by the total number of boys to find that 70% of the boys agreed. She did this for all the categories.

	Boys	**Girls**
Agree	70%	40%
Disagree	30%	60%

Make observations based on this new data display.

Based on these data, it seems that boys are much more likely to agree than girls, because 70% of boys agreed and only 40% of girls agreed.

⊸€ Connect

Jeremy asked a sample of 40 eighth-grade students whether or not they had a curfew. He then asked if they had a set bedtime for school nights. He recorded his data in this two-way frequency table.

	Bedtime	No Bedtime	Total
Curfew	21	4	25
No Curfew	3	12	15
Total	24	16	40

Create a two-way relative frequency table for these data. Does that table show an association between these two variables?

1

Divide the number of "curfew with set bedtime" responses by the total number of students with a set bedtime.

$21 ÷ 24 = 0.875 = 87.5\%$

This shows that 87.5% of students with a set bedtime also have a curfew.

2

Find other relative frequencies and create a table.

	Bedtime	No Bedtime
Curfew	87.5%	25%
No Curfew	12.5%	75%

▶ Based on the table above, it appears that there is an association. Students who have a set bedtime are much more likely to have a curfew, and students who have no curfew are much more likely to have no set bedtime.

CHECK

If the columns of relative frequencies do not add to 100%, there is an error in your calculations. Check that the "bedtime" and "no bedtime" columns add to 100%. Do the rows also add to 100%? If not, explain why not.

Practice

Classify each data set as numerical or categorical.

1. boy, girl, girl, girl, boy

   _____

2. 1, 2, 6, 8, 10, 12, 13.5

   _____

3. voted, didn't vote, voted, didn't vote

   _____

Ten students at lunch were asked which grade they were in and whether or not they played on a school team. Use the results, shown below, for questions 4–8.

Student	Greg	Haley	Ilya	Jen	Kate	Liam	Mike	Nate	Olive	Peg
Grade	6	7	6	6	7	6	7	7	7	6
School Team?	Yes	No	No	No	Yes	No	Yes	Yes	No	Yes

4. Below is an empty two-way frequency table. In which cell would you record Greg's response? Haley's response?

	6th Grade	7th Grade	Total
On a School Team			
Not on a School Team			
Total	5	5	10

   _____

5. Complete the two-way table above. Then use it to make one observation.

   _____

6. What is the relative frequency that a 6th-grade student plays on a sports team? Show your work.

   _____

7. Determine other relative frequencies and complete the two-way frequency table below.

	6th Grade	7th Grade
On a School Team	_____%	_____%
Not on a School Team	_____%	_____%

8. Use the two-way relative frequency table to make an observation about the data.

   _____

Fill in the blanks.

9. The number of times a data point appears in a set is called a _____.

10. _____ categorical data compares two different variables to determine if there is an association.

11. A _____ involves dividing a category's frequency by the sum of all the frequencies for the relevant variable.

Use the data below for questions 12 and 13.

The table shows the grade levels and primary home languages for all the students at Martin Middle School.

	6th Grade	7th Grade	8th Grade	Total
Home Language: English	104	99	116	319
Home Language: Other	56	81	84	221
Total	160	180	200	540

12. **ORGANIZE** Use the grid below to create a two-way relative frequency table for these data.

13. **EXAMINE** After examining the data, would you expect the town from which the middle school draws its students to have a very small or a sizeable population of recent immigrants? Can you say for certain from these data?

_____

_____

_____

For each scatter plot, describe the association shown as linear or nonlinear. If no association is shown, state that.

1.

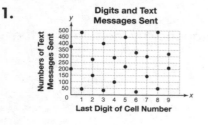

_____

2.

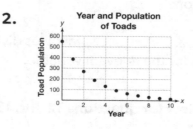

_____

Choose the best answer.

3. The pep club is ordering small, custom flags for students to wave during the playoff game. The price per flag changes depending on the number ordered, as shown in the scatter plot, and is modeled by the function $y = 1 - 0.01x$.

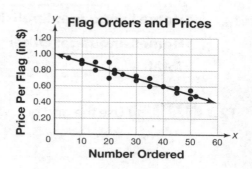

Which is the best interpretation of the y-intercept of this model?

A. The cost for 1 flag will be $0.

B. The cost per flag will generally be less than $1.00.

C. The cost per flag will generally be less than $0.01.

D. The cost per flag will generally be more than $1.00.

4. A coach recorded the times athletes spent weight training and the numbers of sit-ups they could perform in one minute, in the scatter plot to the right. The linear model is $y = 4x + 12$.

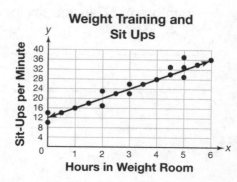

Which is the best interpretation of the slope of this model?

A. Each additional hour in the weight room improves one's performance by 4 sit-ups per minute.

B. Every 4 hours in the weight room improves one's performance by 1 sit-up per minute.

C. An athlete who does not lift weights can perform only 4 sit-ups per minute.

D. The number of hours spent in the weight room does not affect sit-up performance.

For each scatter plot, draw a trend line that fits the data well.

5. This scatter plot shows the ages of cars and their values in dollars.

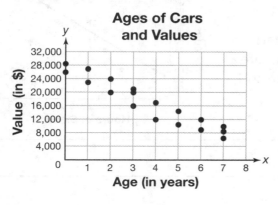

6. This scatter plot shows the number of customers at a farm stand each hour and the total amount collected that hour.

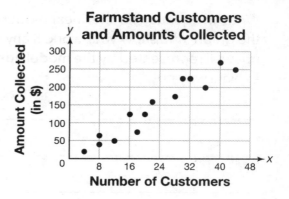

Choose the best answer.

7. A survey of randomly selected eighth-grade students explored the relationship between gender and video game play.

	Boys	Girls	Total
Play Daily	45	12	57
Do Not Play Daily	5	38	43
Total	50	50	100

Which is **not** a reasonable interpretation of the data?

A. More boys surveyed play video games daily than girls.

B. Ignoring gender, a little more than half of the eighth-grade students surveyed play video games daily.

C. Of the boys surveyed, 5% do not play video games daily.

D. Of the girls surveyed, exactly 24% play video games daily.

8. A survey of students in a homeroom class explored the relationship between gender and participation in the school band.

	Boys	Girls	Total
In Band	4	8	12
Not in Band	9	5	14
Total	13	13	26

Which is a reasonable conclusion to draw from these data?

A. There are more band members in the class than non-band members.

B. There are more boys in the class than girls.

C. Among the boys, there are more boys in the band than not in the band.

D. More than one-half of the band members in the class are girls.

Solve.

9. **MODEL** This scatter plot shows the numbers of hours of sleep 14 students got the night before a class presentation and their grades for the assignment.

   Write an equation for the linear model represented by the graph, and show your work. If any data points are not well represented by the model, identify them and explain why not.

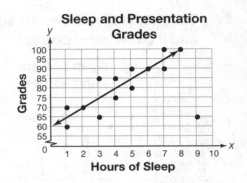

Sleep and Presentation Grades

_____

_____

_____

10. **EXAMINE** The table shows the costs of hats and the numbers of hats sold at a clothing store. Plot the data in the table on the grid. Then draw a trend line for the data and explain how you know your line is a good fit.

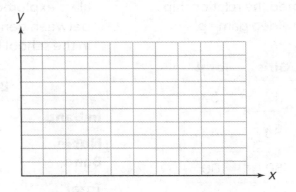

Number Sold

Price of Hat (in $)	5	10	15	20	20	25	25	30	35	40	40	45	45
Number Sold	36	28	32	24	32	20	28	24	12	12	20	8	36

_____

_____

_____

Exploring Variables

Work in small groups or individually. Choose two variables that you would like to explore. You will then survey students in your class, record your data, and create tables to help you analyze it.

For example, if you decide to explore the relationship between gender and lunch, you could record whether a student was a boy or a girl and then ask them if they buy school lunch or bring lunch from home. You do not need to use this example.

I want to explore these two variables: _____ and _____.

Conduct your survey. Use a piece of scrap paper or notebook paper to record students' responses. It is important to write down responses as your classmates will probably be surveying you at the same time. You may ask every student in your class or ask a sample.

Use the blank grids below to construct a two-way frequency table and a two-way relative frequency table for your data.

Frequency Table

			Total
Total			

Relative Frequency Table

	_____%	_____%
	_____%	_____%

Use your tables to make some observations below about the data you collected.

_____

_____

_____

_____

_____

_____

Glossary

alternate exterior angles angles that lie outside parallel lines and on opposite sides of a transversal (Lesson 23)

alternate interior angles angles that lie inside parallel lines and on opposite sides of a transversal (Lesson 23)

base in a power, the number that is used as a factor the number of times indicated by the exponent (Lesson 3)

bivariate data pairs of linked observations (Lesson 29)

coefficient a number multiplied by a variable, or the first factor (a number greater than or equal to 1 and less than 10) in scientific notation (Lesson 5)

coincident lines lines that have all their points in common (Lesson 10)

congruent characteristic of figures that can be made to coincide exactly by a sequence of rigid motions (Lesson 18)

corresponding angles angles that lie on the same side of a transversal and on the same side of parallel lines (Lesson 23)

cube root one of three equal factors of a number (Lesson 4)

dilation a transformation that changes the size of a figure according to a scale factor (Lesson 21)

elimination a method of solving a system of equations algebraically whereby two equations are added or subtracted to remove a variable (Lesson 11)

exponent in a power, the number that indicates how many times the base is used as a factor (Lesson 3)

exterior angle an angle formed by a side of a polygon and an extension of an adjacent side (Lesson 24)

frequency the number of times each value occurs in a data set (Lesson 32)

function a rule that assigns to each input value exactly one output value (Lesson 13)

hypotenuse in a right triangle, the side opposite the right angle (Lesson 25)

image the figure resulting from a transformation (Lesson 18)

interior angle an angle that is on the inside of a polygon and has its vertex formed by two sides of the polygon (Lesson 24)

irrational number a number that cannot be expressed as a terminating or repeating decimal; an irrational number cannot be represented as $\frac{a}{b}$, where a and b are integers and $b \neq 0$. (Lesson 1)

leg in a right triangle, one of the two shorter sides; it is opposite one of the two acute angles. (Lesson 25)

line of best fit a line that models the relationship between two variables in a scatter plot; also called a trend line (Lesson 30)

linear function a function that, when graphed, will produce a straight line (Lesson 15)

nonlinear function a function that, when graphed, will not produce a straight line (Lesson 15)

origin the intersection of the x- and y-axes on a coordinate graph, at the point (0, 0) (Lesson 7)

outlier a data point with a value that is very different from the other data points in the set (Lesson 29)

parallel lines lines that lie in the same plane and never intersect (Lesson 23)

piecewise function a function whose rule changes depending on the input values used; the graph of a piecewise linear function may consist of several segments that do not lie in the same line. (Lesson 17)

principal square root the nonnegative (positive) square root of a number (Lesson 4)

Pythagorean theorem states that the sum of the squares of the lengths of the legs in a right triangle is equal to the square of the length of the hypotenuse (Lesson 25)

quadratic function a function that can be written in the form $y = ax^2 + bx + c$ with $a \neq 0$; the graph of a quadratic function is a curve. (Lesson 17)

rate of change a ratio that compares two quantities; on a linear graph, it is a comparison of the change in y-values of the line to the corresponding change in x-values. (Lesson 7)

rational number a number whose decimal form is a terminating or repeating decimal; a rational number can be represented as $\frac{a}{b}$, where a and b are integers and $b \neq 0$. (Lesson 1)

real number a number with a location on a number line; real numbers are either rational or irrational. (Lesson 1)

reflection a flip of a figure over a point or a line (Lesson 18)

relation a set of ordered pairs (Lesson 13)

relative frequency the frequency of a particular category divided by the sum of all the frequencies; expressed as a percent or a decimal (Lesson 32)

rigid motion a movement of a figure in a plane such that its size and shape do not change (Lesson 18)

rotation a turn of a figure around a point (Lesson 18)

same-side interior angles angles that lie inside parallel lines and on the same side of a transversal (Lesson 23)

scale factor the ratio of the lengths of corresponding sides of two similar figures (Lesson 21)

scatter plot a graph of paired data in which the data values are plotted as points in the (x, y) format (Lesson 29)

scientific notation a way to express very large and very small numbers; in scientific notation, the first factor, the coefficient, is a number that is greater than or equal to 1 and less than 10 and the second factor is a power of 10. (Lesson 5)

similar having the same shape, but not necessarily the same size (Lesson 22)

slope a ratio that compares the change in *y*-coordinates of a graph to the corresponding change in *x*-coordinates; the symbol for slope is *m*. (Lesson 7)

square root one of the two equal factors of a number (Lesson 4)

substitution a method of solving a system of equations algebraically whereby an expression equivalent to a variable is substituted for the variable (Lesson 11)

translation a slide of a figure to a new location (Lesson 18)

transversal a line that intersects two or more lines (Lesson 23)

trend line a line that models the relationship between two variables in a scatter plot; also called a line of best fit (Lesson 30)

unit rate a rate that, when expressed as a fraction, has a denominator of 1 (Lesson 7)

vertical angles when two lines intersect, the angles that are opposite each other (Lesson 23)

y-intercept the point or points at which a graph crosses the *y*-axis (Lesson 8)

Math Tool: Coordinate Planes

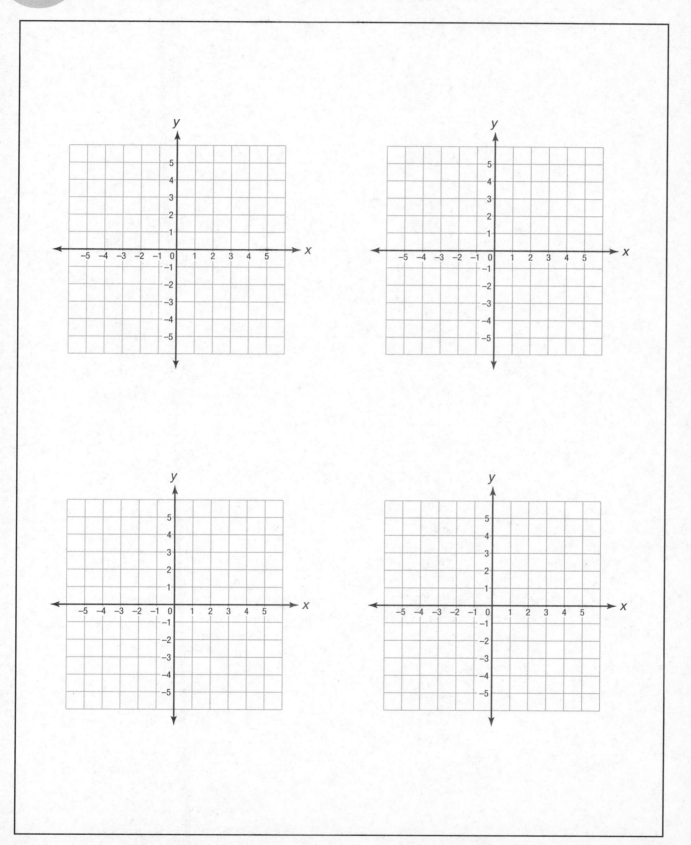

Math Tool: Coordinate Planes

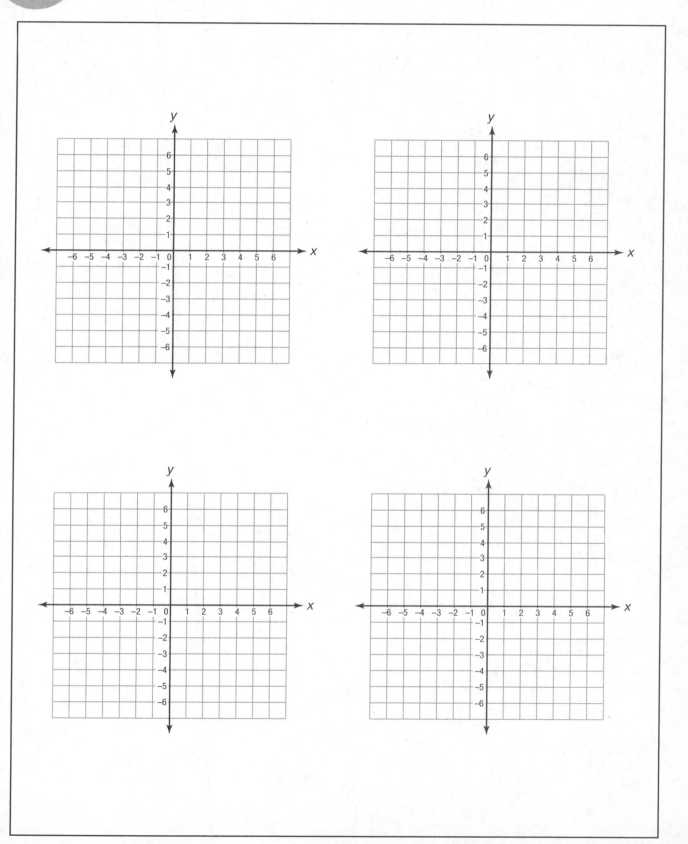

Math Tool: Coordinate Plane

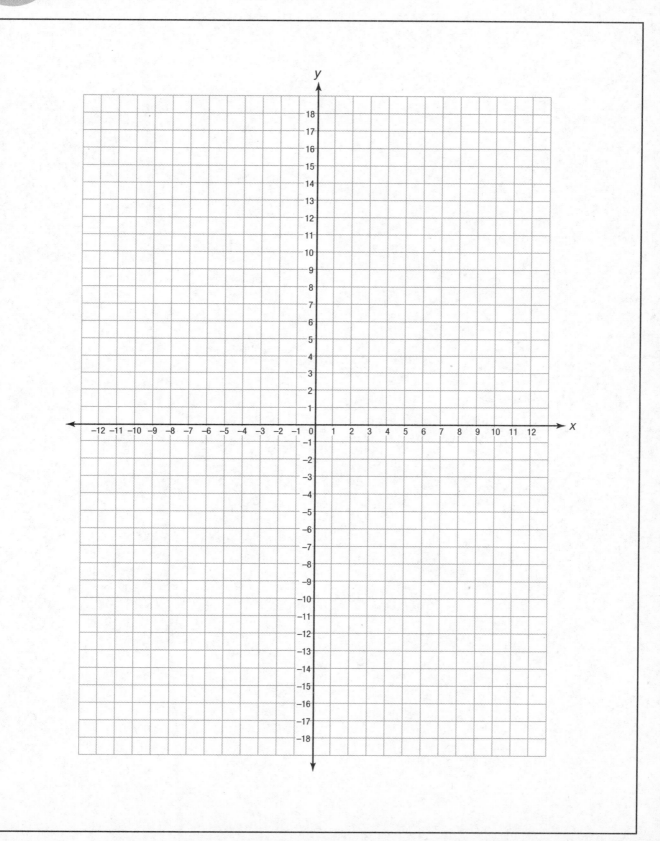

Math Tool: Blank Coordinate Plane

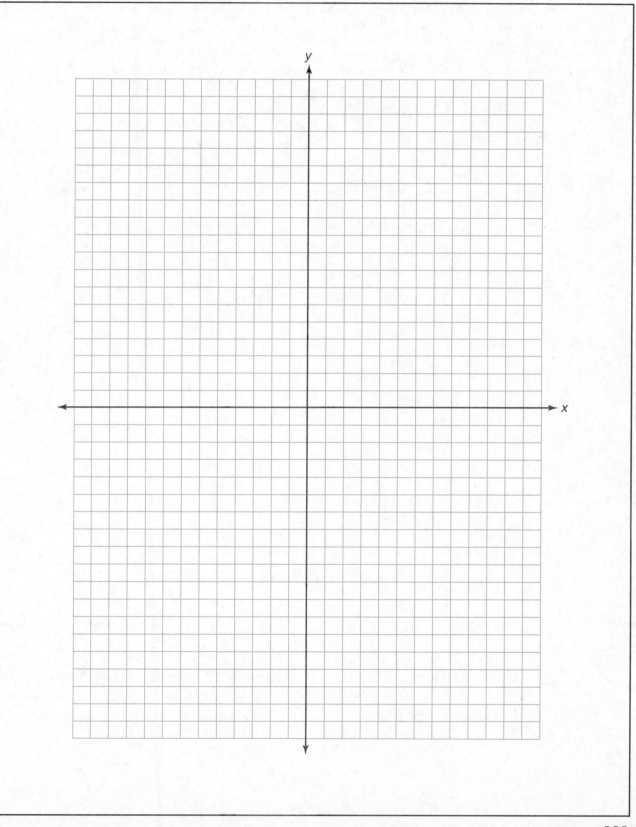

Math Tool: First Quadrant Coordinate Planes

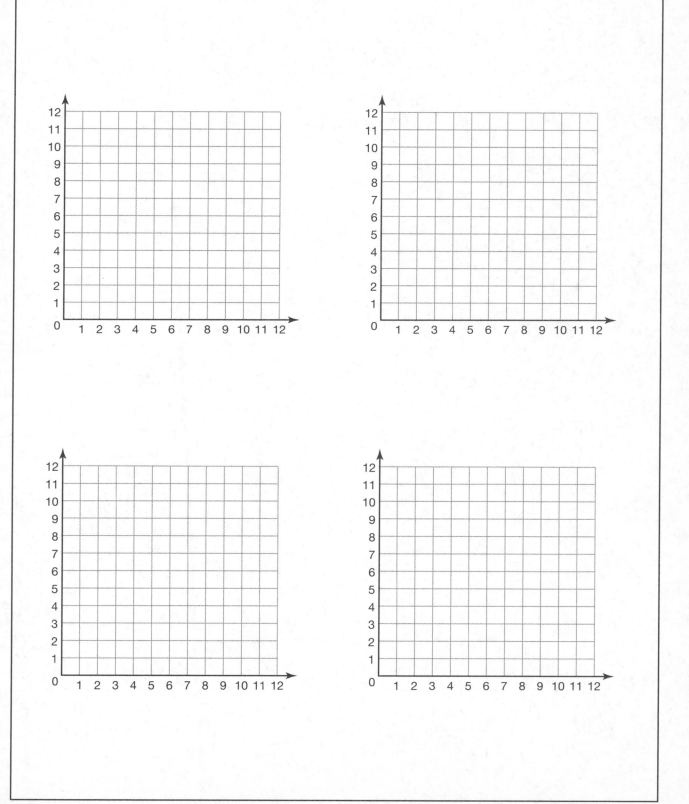

Math Tool: Grid Paper

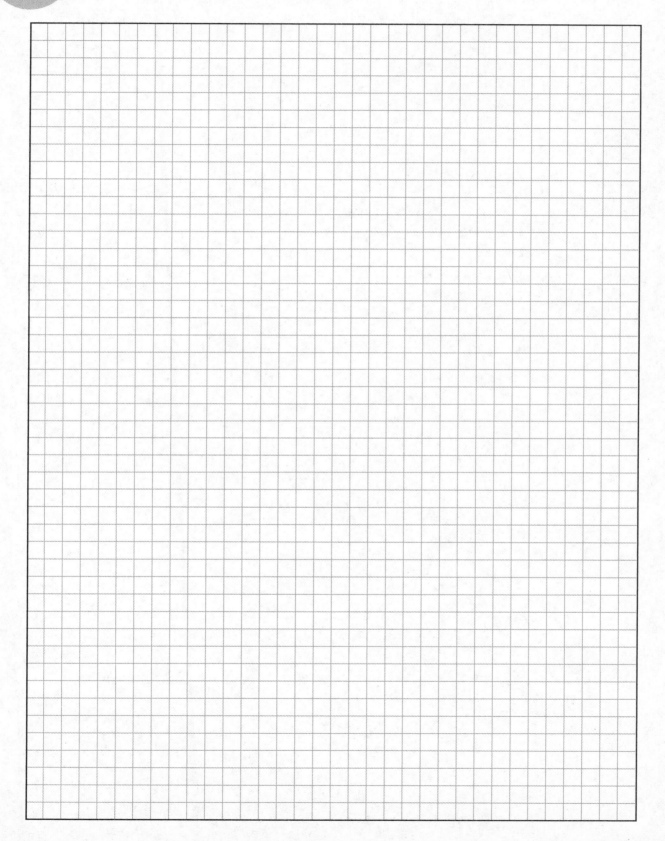

Math Tool: Volume Formulas

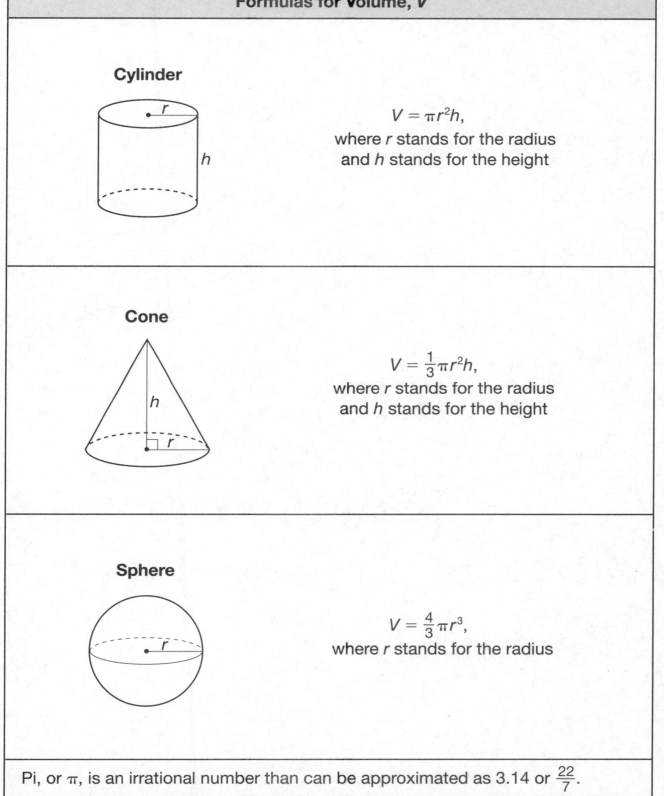

Formulas for Volume, *V*

Cylinder

$$V = \pi r^2 h,$$

where *r* stands for the radius
and *h* stands for the height

Cone

$$V = \frac{1}{3}\pi r^2 h,$$

where *r* stands for the radius
and *h* stands for the height

Sphere

$$V = \frac{4}{3}\pi r^3,$$

where *r* stands for the radius

Pi, or π, is an irrational number than can be approximated as 3.14 or $\frac{22}{7}$.

Math Tool: Pythagorean Theorem Proof

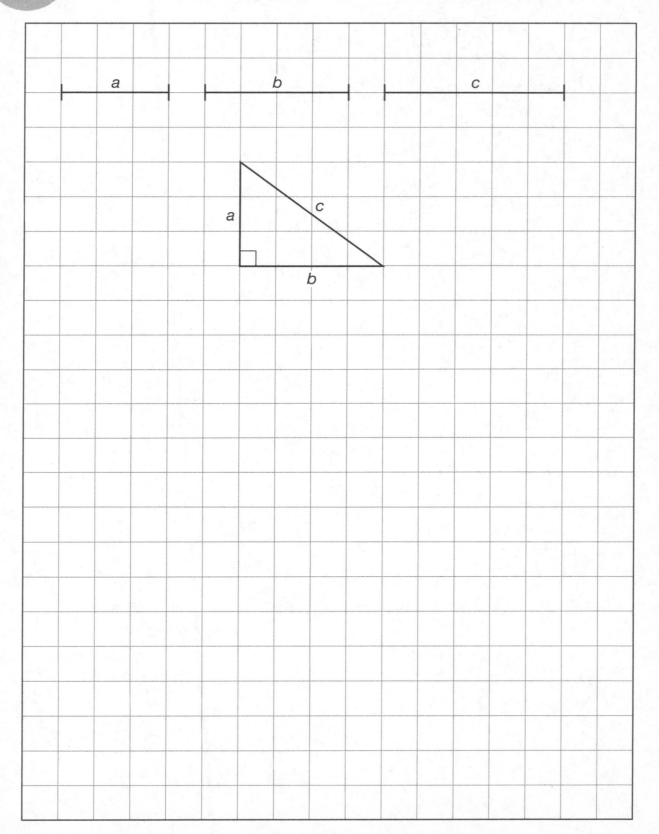

Notes

Notes

Notes

Notes

Notes

Notes

Notes

Notes